Communicative Competence Approaches
to Language Proficiency Assessment:
Research and Application

Multilingual Matters

Please contact us for the latest information on recent and forthcoming books in the series.

Derrick Sharp, General Editor,
Multilingual Matters,
Bank House, 8A Hill Road,
Clevedon, Avon BS21 7HH, England.

MULTILINGUAL MATTERS 9

Communicative Competence Approaches to Language Proficiency Assessment: Research and Application

Edited by
Charlene Rivera

MULTILINGUAL
MATTERS LTD

Multilingual Matters Ltd
Bank House, 8a Hill Road
Clevedon, Avon BS21 7HH
England

British Library Cataloguing in Publication Data

Communicative competence approaches to
language proficiency assessment.
    (Multilingual matters; 9)
1. Language and languages—Ability testing
I. Rivera, Charlene   II. Series
401'.9   P53.4

ISBN 0-905028-22-8
ISBN 0-905028-21-X Pbk

Production co-ordination and jacket design by
MM Productions Ltd, 1 Brookside, Hertford, Herts SG13 7LJ

Typeset by Herts Typesetting Services, Hertford.
Printed and bound in Great Britain by Robert Hartnoll Ltd., Bodmin, Cornwall.

To my family.

Contents

Acknowledgements

This volume would not have been possible without the support of the National Institute of Education and InterAmerica Research Associates. It would not have become a reality without the assistance of many dedicated individuals. It is with much gratitude that they are here recognized.

Reynaldo Macias, the former NIE Assistant Director for Reading and Language Studies and Ellen Rosansky, the first NIE ALPBP Project officer supported the concept of the LPA Symposium and encouraged the formalization of this volume. Dan Ulibarri, who later became the NIE ALPBP Project Officer, also provided invaluable encouragement in its finalization. Carmen Simich-Dudgeon, the ALPBP Research Associate, assisted in the initial conceptualization of the LPA Symposium and through her in depth understanding of the issues which concern bilingual educators and her knowledge of sociolinguistics and ethnography contributed greatly to the volume. Mary Cunningham, the LPA Symposium coordinator, who skillfully handled all of the Symposium logistics, helped to locate interested publishers for the volume. The fruits of her efforts are here realized. Eileen Shaw, the technical editor, spent unending hours reviewing and editing manuscripts. She together with Elizabeth Gannon, who verified all references, provided moral support and encouragement throughout the preparation of this volume.

Finally, I would like to thank the National Academy of Education who through a Spencer Foundation Grant have made it possible for me to dedicate time and resources in the final production of this book.

Charlene Rivera
former ALPBP Project Director

Preface

The great population shifts occurring throughout the world today have focussed attention on language policy in the education of children who do not speak the language of the country in which they are being schooled. The establishment of guest-worker policies in Europe and Australia and politically-motivated migrations of peoples from regions such as Southeast Asia and the Caribbean are some of the events that have brought about this situation. As Kloss observes,

> "Until recently, it was possible to venture an admittedly crude generalization regarding the global issue of language maintenance vs. language shift. Africa and the Americas, so the statement went, were leaning toward language shift in order to reduce the number of tribal tongues, and in the New World, also of immigrant tongues. In Europe and Asia, on the other hand, the psychological climate was held to be more favorable to language retention. This juxtaposition is beginning to get blurred, chiefly because so many American nations are moving toward greater freedom for maintenance — as a concomitant — for the unfolding of nondominant languages." (1977, p. iii)

Although the official language of the Federal government has always been English, historically the United States has not been a strictly monolingual country in either the speech of its people or its governments. State and local polities with high concentrations of people speaking other languages, at various times, have conducted their affairs in languages other than English: Spanish in Puerto Rico, French in some parishes of Louisiana and counties of Maine, German in Pennsylvania and Ohio, and Spanish in the Southwest and New York City.

Current Census data indicate that over 65 languages are spoken by a large number of citizens; recognition of the distinction among the Native

This volume was prepared as part of the Assessment of Bilingual Persons Project supported in part through the National Institute of Education's contract (N.I.E. 400-79-002) with InterAmerica Research Associates. The Opinions of the contributors are their own and do not reflect those of the National Institute of Education.

American languages would add even more. The linguistic diversity brought on by earlier waves of immigration continues today as new waves of Vietnamese, Cambodians and Iranians enter this country (Kloss, 1977). The cost and consequences of the different approaches being used in the United States to educate such children are, therefore, of great interest not only within this country, but also to those concerned with the social, economic and political fabric of many other countries.

Schools have used diverse instructional methods for children from families speaking languages other than English. Some have taught in English in a sink or swim fashion or with the variant of adapting the English used to the students' comprehension. Some combine special tutoring in English, English as a Second Language (ESL), with use of English as the language of the classroom. If the student seems more proficient in the native language than in English, in addition to ESL instruction, some schools provide academic instruction in the student's first language. Still others, particularly in the early grades, provide almost all formal instruction in the students' first language, phasing in ESL while the child becomes literate in the native language.

Decisions about instructional approaches are influenced by considerations other than that of the learner's mastery of English. For example, some major factors considered include the number of language minority students, language diversity, availability of qualified teachers, costs, and attitudes toward language acquisition and maintenance. In making a decision about instructional approaches various theories concerning the nature of language proficiency essential for success in school along with an understanding of the impact of the various instructional approaches on the development of language skills and overall student achievement are important components. Often at the core of such a discussion are beliefs about the what and the how of language proficiency assessment.

The purposes of the Assessment of the Language Proficiency of Bilingual Persons (ALPBP) project were, first, to bring together what is known about these issues and, second, to improve understanding of language proficiency assessment in ways that would be practical for classroom teachers. The result, it was hoped, would be to provide constructs for thinking about language proficiency that could lead to practical tools for teachers' use and to better informed entry/exit decisions.

Points of Origin

There were several points of origin for the ALPBP project. One was the

1978 Falmouth Conference on Testing, Teaching and Learning (Tyler & White, 1979). This conference came about as a result of the 1978 conference called by the Department of Health, Education and Welfare (DHEW) which focused on the reasons for the decline in achievement test scores. Participants at the DHEW conference argued that a significant factor in the decline was the use of inappropriate tests. Using this line of reasoning the Falmouth Conference participants concluded that testing could serve important purposes if it was done in a different manner. They recognized that the use of standardized testing was often inefficient and unreliable, particularly, when used to make educational decisions about individuals and about program effectiveness. This was found to be particularly true in light of findings from human cognition studies. Thus, the participants urged Federal support of new approaches to testing:

> "How are we to pursue this vision of testing merged into a teaching-testing system, fitted to the natural classroom situation, drawing upon the cognitive scientists and teachers and scholars in the subject areas, and exploiting the rapidly developing information-handling technology? One way is to continue and perhaps expand support for research on classroom process and human cognition, and for the development of new technologically-based testing, and testing involving persons from the subject area." (Tyler & White, 1979, p. 12)

Another point of origin was a national survey of language minority students (O'Malley, 1981) and a project to develop entry-exit criteria for bilingual education programs (Southwest, 1980). Despite the usefulness of the results of these projects, their development was marked by some concern for the inadequacy of language proficiency assessment measures. The researchers used the best of what was known in order to carry out the survey and to develop criteria recognized that the time had arrived to put resources into the kind of studies that could contribute to the overall improvement of language proficiency assessment procedures, a view supported by many researchers (e.g. Cazden et al., 1972; Cummins, 1979; Carrasco et al., 1978; Hymes, 1976).

A third point of origin was the enthusiasm shown by many involved in language proficiency assessment for what variously had been called interactive research, collaborative development and developmental research. The notion is that knowledge and application have for too long been separated. More effective research, it has been recognized, can be carried out if researchers and practitioners work together as co-equal members of a team. A few models of such interactive research have been carried out (e.g. Tikunoff *et al.*, 1979; Tikunoff *et al.*, 1980; Philips, 1980; Shalaway & Lanier, 1979) and their results seem promising.

Other points of origin were the thinking that went into research agenda-building for the 1978 Congressionally mandated bilingual education studies, the funding of the Center for Research on Bilingualism, and the bilingual research concerns of the National Institute of Education's Teaching and Learning Program. The scores of papers, workshops, analyses, conferences and meetings leading into these activities laid some of the foundations for the project.

The issues which emerged from these activities and experiences precipitated NIE to develop an RFP which called for interactive research and which focused on issues related to language proficiency assessment. The RFP states that,

> "Two of the most pressing needs in educating children from minority language backgrounds are (1) to pursue fundamental research on the nature of language proficiency and how it can be measured, and (2) to provide teachers with up-to-date knowledge of language proficiency assessment so they can improve their classroom assessment practices. The purpose of the RFP is to solicit proposals for a program of work with two parts: (1) the administration of a competitive research program to support fundamental research on language proficiency assessment and (2) the operation of an experimental program of teacher training designed to introduce teachers to current research perspectives on language proficiency assessment." (NIE, 1979, p. 5)

Arrivals

How successful has the effort been?

First, educational decisions are not likely to be better than our understanding of language acquisition, language functioning and the nature of language and its uses. While the finest crucible for promoting understanding may be theory-based, hypothesis-testing strong inference studies, another way of assessing depth of understanding is to determine if it can be applied. In this sense, the project has been successful.

Second, one of the functions of research is to help illuminate the way issues are thought about. It should improve ability to speak in more precise terms, and to refine the debates that go on as people seek their way toward new policies. Although a consensus on what is known about the nature of language proficiency and how it can be measured may not have been reached, the ALPBP project effort should at least clarify points of disagreement, reasons for them, and frame the issues even more constructively. Here also the results were commensurate with the considerable effort invested in the ALPBP project.

Third, the effort to form a working definition of communicative competence and language proficiency and to make practical recommendations which would be useful to teachers in the assessment of language minority students for the purpose of making better entry/exit decisions and for the improvement of classroom practice. Here our reach exceeded our grasp and the fundamental research. Although many definitions and descriptions are offered in the papers in this volume, it was not possible to reach a consensus with regard to a working definition of communicative competence.

Determining how many children in this country are language minority, deciding which of their needs are uniquely language related, and what services may meet those needs are tasks which are likely to engage attention for some time to come. Definitions and their applications may influence estimates of resources needed, distribution of resources, and the nature of programs, as well as the fate of individual students. Hoping for clean-cut guidance on any of these issues is ambitious. They are, however, all important and the ALPBP project seems to have brought together the most that good research, carefully and creatively pursued, can offer at this time.

Lois-ellin Datta
former Associate Director
NIE Program in Teaching
and Learning

Notes
1. Opinions are the author's and do not represent the position of the National Institute of Education.

References

Carrasco, R. L., Vera, A., & Cazden, C. V. 1978, Aspects of bilingual students' communicative competence in the classroom: A case study. Paper presented at the National Conference on Chicano and Latino Discourse Behavior, Princeton, N.J.

Cazden, C., John, V., & Hymes, D. (eds) 1972, *Functions of language in the classroom*. New York: Teachers College Press.

Cummins, J. 1979, Linguistic interdependence and the educational development of bilingual children. *Review of Educational Research*, 49(2), 222–51.

Hymes, D. 1976, Ethnographic measurement. Paper presented at the Symposium on Language Development in a Bilingual Setting, Pamona, CA.

Kloss, H. 1977, *The American bilingual tradition.* Rowley, Mass.: Newbury House Publishers.

National Institute of Education, 1979, Assessing the language proficiency of bilingual persons (RFP No. NIE-R-79-0012). Washington, D.C.

O'Malley, J. M. 1981, *Children's English and services study: Language minority children with limited English proficiency in the United States.* Washington, D.C.: National Clearinghouse for Bilingual Education.

Philips, D. 1980, What do the researcher and the practitioner have to offer each other? *Educational Researcher,* 9(11), 17–20; 24.

Shalaway, L. & Lanier, J. 1979, Teachers collaborate in research. *New England Teacher Corps Exchange,* 2(3), 1–2.

Southwest Regional Laboratory for Educational Research and Development. 1980, *Resources for developing a student placement system for bilingual programs.* Washington, D.C.: U.S. Department of Health, Education and Welfare.

Tikunoff, W. J., Ward, B. A. & Griffin, G. A. 1979, *Interactive research and development on teaching* (Final report). San Francisco, CA: Far West Regional Laboratory.

Tikunoff, W. J., Ward, B. A. & Lazar, C. 1980, Partners: Teachers, researchers, trainer/developers – An interactive approach to teacher education R & D. In D. E. Hall, S. M. Hord & B. Brown (eds), *Exploring issues in teacher education: Questions for future research.* Austin, TX: The Research and Development Center for Teacher Education.

Tyler, R. W. & White, S. J. 1979, *Testing, teaching and learning.* Washington, D.C.: U.S. Department of Health, Education and Welfare.

Background to the language proficiency assessment symposium

This and the accompanying three volumes are composed of selected papers which were presented at the Language Proficiency Assessment Symposium (LPA), held March 14–18, 1981, at the Airlie House Conference Center in Warrenton, Virginia. The Symposium was planned and implemented as a component of the Assessment of Language Proficiency of Bilingual Persons (ALPBP) project. The goals of the ALPBP project, funded by the National Institute of Education (NIE, 1979) and administered by InterAmerica Research Associates, Inc., were:

— to pursue fundamental research on the nature of language proficiency and how it can be measured; and
— to provide teachers with up-to-date knowledge of language proficiency assessment (issues) so they can improve their classroom assessment practices (p. 5).

The LPA Symposium represented a major effort toward integrating both the insights gained from findings emerging from the research component and the implementation of the teacher training programs of the ALPBP project. The Symposium provided a forum where a broad spectrum of researchers, practitioners, and policymakers met to discuss the major issues and research findings which affect language proficiency assessment practices.

Researchers were represented by scholars involved in the development of models of communicative competence, related empirical research, and the development and validation of tests of language proficiency and/or communicative competence. Practitioners included teachers and school administrators engaged in the implementation of programs which require the application of language proficiency assessment strategies. Policymakers were individuals who play an important role in the funding of education research projects related to language proficiency assessment and who are influential in the establishment of policy in this area.

The participants interacted through the presentation of papers, reactions to presentations, and informal discussions. The main goals of the Symposium were selected by the organizers based on the issues identified in a survey of researchers and educators.

The goals were:

— to develop a working definition of communicative proficiency;
— to make recommendations for the assessment of language minority students for the purpose of entry/exit into appropriate educational programs; and
— to make recommendations for further research and to develop a research agenda.

In regard to the first goal, the Symposium participants acknowledged the need to clarify the nature and scope of communicative proficiency and its relationship to language proficiency. It was evident that some agreement among researchers and practitioners, along with much more conclusive information about the nature of language and how it should be measured, would be necessary to clarify the concepts. However, the recognized knowledge gaps and the diversity of perspectives, theories and research findings concerning the nature of language and its measurement, prevented the LPA Symposium participants from reaching a consensus. Issues which relate to this topic are found in this volume, *Communicative Competence Approaches to Language Proficiency Assessment: Research and Application.* The issues discussed range from theoretical questions regarding the construct of communicative proficiency to research relating communicative proficiency to literacy related skills. Language tests and testing methodologies are considered in several papers. Questions are raised as to what tests should be measuring and why. The reliability of currently-used language proficiency assessment instruments, as well as the development of new, more appropriate measures are also addressed.

Issues related to the second goal are found in this and the subsequent three volumes. *An Ethnographic Sociolinguistic Approach to Language Proficiency Assessment* takes a multidisciplinary approach to language proficiency assessment and supports the development of innovative methods for analyzing patterns of children's language use. The research presented involves what has been called ethnographic/sociolinguistic approaches which places emphasis on the understanding of language use through the observation of children's language in naturally-occurring contexts. These approaches are in contrast to the use of traditional testing and experimental research methodologies.

The relationship between a learner's first and second language development and performance in school are the focus of the volume *Language Proficiency and Academic Achievement*. "A major reason for the confused state of the art of language proficiency in bilingual programs . . . stems from the failure to develop an adequate theoretical framework for relating language proficiency to academic achievement," argues Cummins. He contends that without such a "framework it is impossible either to develop rational entry/exit criteria for bilingual programs or to design testing procedures to assess these criteria". The validity of the framework proposed by Cummings is debated in the volume.

The concerns of practitioners, researchers and policymakers, which relate to the assessment and placement of language minority students in bilingual education programs, are the theme of the volume *Placement Procedures in Bilingual Education: Education and Policy Issues*. The volume focuses on the legal and practical implications of federal guidelines with regard to language proficiency assessment practices.

In meeting the third goal, the LPA Symposium provided a structure for participants to make practical recommendations directed at influencing federal and state policies regarding language proficiency assessment research and practices. The papers in all four volumes represent the participants' understanding of the various issues. The following is a summary of the conclusions reached and the recommendations made by the three groups represented at the Symposium — researchers, practitioners and policymakers.

The primary concerns of the researchers were:

— The need for basic research into the nature of language that can provide the foundation for clarifying the concept of communicative competence and its relationship to language proficiency;
— The need for applied research that expands on current understanding of the state of the art of language proficiency assessment;
— The need to undertake validation studies of currently available language proficiency assessment instruments;
— The development of multiple language assessment strategies that include both quantitative and qualitative components;
— The need for adaptable government guidelines that affect language proficiency assessment practices;
— The need for yearly meetings between researchers and practitioners to exchange information and ideas.

The major issues identified by the practitioners were:

— The need for a working definition of communicative competence that clarifies its relationship to language proficiency;
— The establishment of practical as well as adaptable federal guidelines affecting language proficiency assessment practices;
— The importance of maintaining a network of communication between practitioners and researchers;
— The importance of obtaining up-to-date information on language proficiency assessment practices through more extensive use of resources such as the National Clearinghouse for Bilingual Education (NCBE);
— The use of the LPA Symposium as a model for future meetings among practitioners, researchers and policymakers involved in language proficiency assessment practices that affect minority language students;
— The support of federal agencies in encouraging collaborative research, an example of which would be including as criteria in Requests for Proposals (RFPs) the participation of practitioners at the local level.

The issues of most importance, as seen by the policymakers, were:

— The need to establish federal guidelines that can be adapted to accommodate relevant research findings that have bearing on the application of language proficiency assessment practices;
— The need to establish federal guidelines that can be adapted to to support applied research on issues related to language proficiency assessment through grants and other forms of funding;
— The need for federal agencies to support research that is carried out as a joint venture on the part of researchers and practitioners.

The question of whether or not the objectives of the LPA Symposium were attained remains to be seen. It is hoped that the papers presented in the four volumes will add new insights into the issue of language proficiency assessment. It is believed that the research and theoretical perspectives offered will represent a positive step toward attaining the development of effective language proficiency assessment procedures and, ultimately, a more equitable education for language minority students in the United States.

Charlene Rivera

Visiting Scholar
NAEP Project
Educational Testing service

Introduction

The focus of this volume is on those theoretical, psychometric and practical issues which pose a challenge to the measurement of language proficiency. The complexity and difficulty of defining communicative competence and identifying valid and appropriate approaches for its measurement among students with limited English skills is reflected both by the researchers and educators who contributed to the volume.

The plan of the book

The book is divided into two sections which demonstrate the need for continued multidisciplinary dialogue among researchers and practitioners. In particular, the variation in perspectives and approaches calls attention to critical issues of concern to bilingual educators which reflect some of the following issues:

— What is the relationship between language proficiency and communicative competence?
— How does communicative competence relate to academic achievement?
— Are there some common themes in the research reported here that provide insight both for researchers attempting to develop new language proficiency measures as well as for practitioners currently relying on currently available ones?

Approaches to Communicative Competence

This part of the book centers on current perspectives and research. The individual chapters in their diversity, pose a challenge both for those attempting to use communicative competence to interpret the results of currently used language proficiency measures as well as for those attempting to develop valid language assessment instruments from a communicative competence perspective.

Wallat in, "An Overview of Communicative Competence", provides a history of the development of communicative competence and its influence in the "study of teaching, learning and performance". The significant feature of communicative competence, she indicates, is the social component or "how individuals convey social information about the situation they perceive is being constructed . . . (and) how the individual acts under the assumption that the other person shares the same expectations about what is being said and what context they are building".

From a psychometric perspective Bachman and Palmer describe three approaches to language proficiency assessment in their article, "Some Comments on the Terminology of Language Testing". The methods include the skill component approach, the communicative approach and the measurement approach. The authors extensively discuss the measurement approach, through which they indicate it to be possible to describe "what constitutes linguistic competence, language skill, linguistic performance, communicative performance and measures of linguistic and communicative performance". They illustrate their perspective by providing an interpretation of the Canale and Swain model of communicative competence. This description, they indicate, "is consistent with what language tests measure and constitutes a statement of what (is) a reasonable set of hypotheses about the nature of language ability."

Duran, like Wallat, approaches the issue of communicative competence from a sociolinguistic perspective. He argues that attention to discourse and interactional skills may help to improve the interpretation and theoretical design of integrative measures of communicative competence. In the chapter, "Some Implications of Communicative Competence Research for Integrative Proficiency Testing". he provides a rationale for integrating this outlook into new "clinical" techniques of language assessment.

Application

The attempt to better understand communicative competence has resulted in a wide range of applied research within the context of bilingual and immersion education. The chapters, included here are representative of the research undertaken to explore practical and valid ways to assess language competencies and to define their role in the educational placement of students with limited English skills.

Older immigrant students whose first language is better developed upon arrival into a country will acquire English academic skills more rapidly than younger immigrant students. This hypothesis of interdependence was the pivot for the Cummins, *et al.* study, "Linguistic Interdependence Among Japanese and Vietnamese Immigrant Students." The study was designed to test predictions that in an educational context the development of language or communicative proficiencies in L_2 (second language) are partially dependent upon the level of development of L_1 (first language) proficiency. The study findings support the interdependence hypothesis and provide evidence that communicative proficiency is not a static entity, but is part of a multifaceted process of development.

Ramirez's study, "Pupil Characteristics and Performance on Linguistic and Communicative Language Measures", like Cummins' study, highlights the need to understand the relationship between school achievement and language proficiency. Specifically, he examines the predictive validity of linguistic and communicative competence measures as compared with actual student achievement.

In "A Communicative Approach to Language Proficiency Assessment in a Minority Setting", Canale describes an ongoing project to develop two communicative proficiency instruments for use in French language schools. The framework for the instruments (also discussed by Bachman and Palmer) is multifaceted and includes consideration of grammatical competence, sociolinguistic competence, discourse competence and strategic competence.

Bruck, in the final chapter in this section, focuses attention on the acquisition of communicative competence and its relationship to academic achievement of learning disabled students in immersion education programs in Canada. In "The Suitability of Immersion Education for Children with Special Needs", she poses the question: Would learning disabled students educated in a weaker language have the same or similar learning problems if schooled in their native language? The chapter provides insight into those components of instruction in a second language that may be appropriate for this special group of students.

Genesee's chapter, "Psycholinguistic Aspects", concludes the volume. Here Genesee describes basic assumptions about communicative competence and points out that "if language assessment techniques are to keep stride with evolving perspectives in linguistics, sociolinguistics and psychology, they will have to incorporate aspects of communication, however ultimately defined". Like the other authors, he reconfirms the need to clarify the nature of communicative competence and its relationship to language proficiency. Thus in addition to adding, highlighting, positing or negating current findings and perspectives regarding communicative competence, the perspectives represented in the volume provide valuable information about the nature of children's language use, its assessment and the role of first and second language in academic achievement.

PART I

Approaches to
Communicative Competence

An overview of communicative competence

Cynthia Wallat
The Florida State University

The major-purpose of this paper is to review current perspectives and research on socialization and language in educational settings and to present several new images of children and youth's communicative competence.

The four sections that are included in this paper are linked by the use of an illustrative model for the study of classrooms. The major classes of the model provide a way of thinking about how far we have come in the study of teaching, learning and performance.

Section one provides a historical context on the notion of competence and, more specifically, creates a framework for the discussion of current perspectives on communicative competence in section two.

Section three, Extending Our Observation System, suggests how what is currently known about social skill demands in the classroom, psycho-social maturity demands, and instructional setting demands can begin to address Hymes' (1979) argument that developments in our understanding of the concept of competence depend upon becoming more aware of the types of demands we do and do not make on language use in the course of our lives.

In the final section several studies of the range of classroom language demands that are possible in classrooms are reviewed. The studies were selected because of their potential for answering the recognized need to consider the importance of the social situation in assessing communicative performance.

Perspectives on learning and performance

Historically, educators and researchers have been concerned with the notion of what makes an individual academically competent. Psychologists have set themselves the task of explaining the "orderly acquisition of progressively more complex operations that are supposed to ensure that each child attain, without too much difficulty, a level of competency required for success at school" (Perret-Clermont, 1980, p. v). As one developmental psychologist has pointed out:

"Languages exist because of the functions they serve, and so how individuals learn to use language for such different purposes as to get and give information and initiate and monitor interactions with others is a major aspect of development" (Bloom, 1978, p. 1)

It is at this point that social psychologists, sociologists and anthropologists step in and remind us of another regularity which characterizes major aspects of development in our society: the fact that many children do not pass through our school systems with an orderly progression of success (Perret-Clermont, 1980).

Within this sphere of debate regarding learning, the notions of linguistic competence, psycho-social competence, communicative competence, and interactional competence have been addressed in the child development, the ethnography of communication, and the study of teaching literature. The sections that follow describe major aspects or perspectives on competence that have emerged in each of these areas. The review of approaches to competence from child development, social psychology, ethnology, and education research traditions will be provided to establish a historical perspective on the notion of competence, and, more specifically, to provide a current perspective to a model for the study of classroom teaching.

An illustrative model

In 1974 an extensive review of research on teaching and learning was compiled by Michael Dunkin and Bruce Biddle. In order to organize the difficult job of looking back over hundreds of observational studies of classrooms that were conducted in schools between the end of the nineteenth century and the early 1970's, Dunkin & Biddle had to make several decisions. The first decision was how to contend with the same problem that faces all developmental researchers, that is, to find a way of assembling multiple concepts and information in such a way that educators can be reminded about what educators have learned about teaching and what events of teaching (i.e. units of analysis) have been studied.

Dunkin & Biddle solved the problem of presenting information about what was known about teaching up to 1971, and what teaching events had been studied the most up until 1971, by relying on an approach that has become one of the most frequent activities that scientists engage in: model building. The assumption that underlies model building is that in order to monitor anything one needs tools such as a list of traits, or a chart or other visual representation of the whole system or subsystem that is being monitored. Thus Dunkin & Biddle's presage, context, process, and product model of the study of classroom teaching included a wide variety of terms for expressing what was known in the first 70 years of research on the behavior and characteristics of teachers and pupils.

Appropriately, Dunkin & Biddle pointed out that the behavior and characteristics model they constructed was neither exhaustive nor definitive. That is, they did not argue that their model for the study of classroom teaching represents the actual causal processes in the situation. Rather Dunkin & Biddle suggested that models can serve as a tool for individuals who are convinced that it is known: (a) that classroom teaching obviously varies depending on subject, grade level, and group or individual task context, and at the same time recognize that it is also known (b) that within this variation there are similarities or rules for classroom discipline and procedure that hold across grade levels whenever it is found that classroom discourse is conducted using the language of the community.

In building a strong case for the value of continuing the tradition of using new models as tools for the study of classroom teaching, Dunkin & Biddle did not address how their model could incorporate bilingual teaching and learning. As described above, available knowledge as of 1971 when Dunkin & Biddle began their seminal review of the study of classroom interaction had only led to agreement on the finding that similarities in rules for classroom discipline and procedures across grade levels and task contexts can be observed when classroom discourse and the language of the community are one and the same.

In the few short years since Dunkin & Biddle reviewed the findings of the first 70 years of the study of teaching it has been made clear through sponsored research and through educational capacity building funding policies that this nation can no longer be considered a homogeneous monolingual state, and that educators can no longer fail to consider settings that were neglected in the first 70 years of teaching and learning research. Several major unanswered questions that are associated with the issue of bilingualism and past neglect of nonstandard curricula classrooms, rural classrooms, urban classrooms, classrooms for exceptional children, and classrooms representing various ethnic minorities, have been identified. Specifically, these questions are:

"What is the effect of simultaneous membership in several distinct speech communities on the learning and display of communicative skills in a variety of educational situations? What strategies are used by bilingual/bicultural children in learning such skills? Are these strategies alike or different when compared to the development in children from a more homogeneous linguistic background?" (Garnica & King, 1979, p. xvii)

As shown in Figure 1, the model for the study of classroom teaching and learning constructed by Dunkin & Biddle does not include explicit reference to communicative characteristics, causes, or consequences. Yet this model can still accomplish its original purpose which was to organize information in such a way that educators can build on what is known and, at the same time, address questions raised since the early 1970's.

"As may be seen, there are several regions in the model. The central region is the classroom itself, symbolized, . . . by a rectangle. To the left of the classroom are three sets of variables that will surely have at least some influence on classroom events: variables associated with the teacher, variables associated with pupils, and variables representing the context of community, school, and classroom. To the right are some of the hoped for products of education.
Throughout the model appears arrows. Each presumes a causative relationship. . . . Each arrow is but a source of hypotheses, however, and not a symbol of invariant truth." (Dunkin & Biddle, 1974, p. 36)

Current perspectives on strengthening a model for the study of classroom teaching

Following Dunkin & Biddle the thirteen classes of variables suggested in the model reproduced in Figure 1 will be reduced to four larger classes. Following the terminology suggested by Mitzel in 1960, and adopted by Dunkin & Biddle in 1974, presage, context, process, and product variables will be distinguished throughout the remainder of this paper.

Presage variables

Dunkin & Biddle use the term presage variables to include formative experiences and training experiences, as well as measurable personality characteristics teachers take with them into the teaching situation. Recent reviews (Green & Wallat, 1979; 1981; Wallat & Green, 1979; 1982) of the

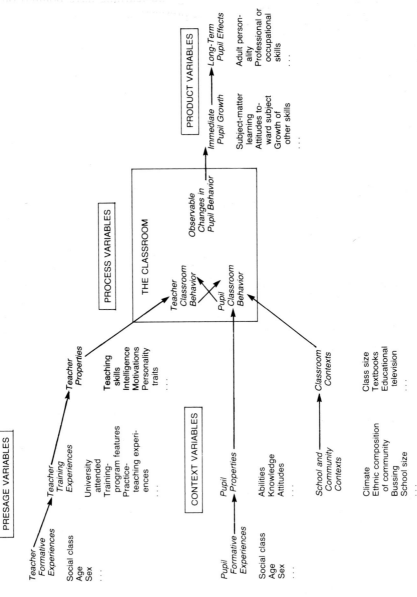

FIGURE 1 A model for the study of classroom teaching. (Dunkin & Biddle, 1974)

significant contributions of many individuals who have contributed to developing new perspectives on teaching and learning have pointed out that the meaning and significance of the presage variables listed in Figure 1 is no longer taken for granted. Although most educators are probably still convinced that the variables Dunkin & Biddle synthesized from past studies on formative experience, training experience, and teacher properties can still help them make some decisions about recruitment and certification, most are also convinced that a model with straight arrows doesn't quite capture the variables affecting a teacher's classroom behavior.

In keeping with the argument that a model for the study of communicative competence in classroom teaching should build on past work it is not suggested here that the presage variables listed in Figure 1 should be ignored. Rather it is suggested that the meaning of formative experiences, training experiences, and propertries will eventually change as evidence mounts regarding why day to day communicative experiences and skills require as much attention in the study of teaching, learning and performance as the "olde" variables we tend to think of as ones that operate long ago before college or before pre-service training. Presage variables identified in Dunkin & Biddle's synthesis of 70 years of research will be amplified, expanded and sometimes altered as language research alerts educators to a range of variables not previously considered. In short, as evidence mounts regarding the assessment value of combining the strengths of traditional sociometric instruments with methods of observing day to day teacher student interactions, the range and scope of meanings associated with presage variables will expand (Foster & Ritchey, 1979; Garnica & King, 1979; Cherry-Wilkinson, 1981).

Building on the work of social psychologists and sociologists one perspective on teacher characteristics that appears useful in a discussion of communicative competence is the view that socialization is a life long interactional process. One interaction paradigm of socialization posits that:

"the phenomenon of socialization can only by understood if seen as a complex interaction process governed by [the pragmatic behavioral effects] of needs, demands, and perspectives. In other words, rather than treating the adult's behavior as an independent variable, both the behavior of adults and of children must be seen as mutually dependent variables" (Dreitzel, 1973, p. 6).

The question is, of course, how can one account for pragmatic (behavior) effects on the part of both the adult and child in a model that includes 3 seemingly different parts called formative experiences, training, and personality characteristics. Tannen's (1979) recent work suggests a way to answer this question. Future studies of teacher's communicative styles in bilingual classrooms can be enriched if guided by the image of teaching as a dual process. The theoretical rationale developed in Tannen's work on conversational style and conversation as a dual process is based on recognition of the need for balanced assessment of the impact of the conversation on both parties (p. 13). The premises that Tannen has been developing include (a) that communicating and learning to communicate always go hand in hand; (b) that just as one cannot not communicate; one cannot not communicate a style; and (c) that individuals are always learning from others and signalling to others *what* it is appropriate to talk about (e.g. notions of appropriate content, and new formulatic phrases that can be used in a social context) and *how* it is appropriate to talk about it (e.g. notions of appropriate extent of camaraderie or distance/deference strategies to apply in a given situation.

The work of Tannen and others (Gumperz & Tannen, 1979) has shown that the distinction between understanding and misunderstanding is an idealized one. In actual interaction speakers and listeners achieve varying degrees of understanding of each others intentions and linguistic devices (p. 31).

The finding that any device (i.e. lexical choices and particular use of paralinguistic features of speech) can fail to establish rapport, or distance, or whatever its user's intention, when used between speakers who are not accustomed to its use for that purpose has been shown by Tannen to occur not only for speakers of different linguistic and cultural backgrounds but among a half dozen friends who all spoke the same language during a Thanksgiving celebration at one friend's home.

"In other words, each person used a unique mix of conversational devices which constituted individual style. When their devices matched, communication between or among them was smooth. When they differed, communication showed signs of disruption or outright mis-undertstanding" (p. 225).

The implications of Tannen work for notions of both the teacher's and the student's communicative competence are significant. She has shown that educators need to consider the finding that communicative competence or conversational style is not composed of discrete categories, but rather dimensions. What can be done in order to eventually strengthen a model of classroom teaching and learning is first, identify how devices such as overlap, pace, silence, persistence, and personal and impersonal topics tend to cluster, and, second, consider the positive or negative expectations, or formative frames, that individuals construct, modify, or suspend about these clusters in different social settings.

Needless to say, the recent findings about the pragmatic (behavior) effects and consequences of devices (Gumperz & Tannen, 1979) requires a change in thinking about how individual and social differences are signaled and evaluated in face to face interaction between parents and children; teachers and children; a parent, teacher and child; and even between colleagues in school and other social institutional settings.

Dell Hymes (1979) has argued for some time that the key to implementing such changes lies primarily in three ingredients:

(a) training in a specialization he has called educational linguistics
(b) influencing the training and outlook of others, and
(c) continuing cooperation between educators and linguists.

Hymes builds his case for reconsidering presage variables by describing the need for changes in the way educators understand the role of language in society and the way they now view competence. He points out that the "old dichotomies . . . correct vs. incorrect, rational vs. emotional, referential vs. expressive, fail to capture . . . the character of competence in relation to the social history and social structure that shape it in a given case" (pp. 9–10). In order to capture and assess the character of competence, training experiences would focus teachers on recent work which questions how formative experiences are thought about. According to Hymes:

"The concern to develop the full potential of each child would lead to recognition of language as involving more than the forms of standard language. . . . When we consider where a child is in his/her development and what his/her potential is, we are considering abilities for which 'competence' is an excellent word. The point is to under- stand the term 'competence' as something close to its ordinary sense, mastery of the use of language" (p. 14, 16).

In order to stimulate new ways of thinking about formative experi- ences, Hymes presents several problems and unanswered questions that he recognizes are difficult for schools to accept. For example educators have yet to come to grips with the findings that:

"there is a pervasive dominant attitude that discourages verbal fluency and expressiveness in white males. It ought to be more widely recognized that in most known societies it is men who are considered the masters of verbal style, and indeed often trained in its ways . . . In our own country, . . . , it is commonly girls who show most verbal ability, who learn or retain foreign languages. . . . Men in public life whose work depends on use of language may be heard to disclaim any special knowledge or command of it" (p. 14)

Hymes raises several additional serious questions and considerations in his discussion of adults communicative competence in our society. First he asks, what is the fate of narrative skill in our society?

"There is some reason to believe . . . that the expressivity of traditional narrative styles has often been disapproved by the upward-ly mobile persons and the middle-class more generally. One sees a loss over several generations of a vital narrative style. . . . People continue to relate accounts and narratives, but are we storying more and enjoying it less?" (p. 14)

A second serious consideration for thinking about formative experi-ences and teacher properties in a model of classroom competency is, according to Hymes, bound up with a limited notion of competence. A valid notion of competence will not come from searching for basic components, but from searching for ways of seeing "the nature of language situations and verbal practices in the United States" (p. 16). Hymes suggests that individuals concerned with understanding their own forma-tive experiences, training experiences, and current skills consider questions such as:

(a) What are the meanings and values associated with the use of language in different age groups and different sectors of profes-sional groups in our society?
(b) What is the fit (and misfit) between abilities and settings — where is an ability frustrated for lack of a setting, or a setting unentered for lack of an ability?
(c) How are the patterns of one's own personal verbal ability shaped or influenced by one's own expectations or frame regarding who can be approached or what settings should be avoided?
(d) How are the patterns of one's own personal ability shaped or influenced by culturally supported aspirations of your own net-work of friends and colleagues?

Context variables

The questions raised by Hymes point to the recent recognition that school and community contexts can no longer continue to be ignored or treated as only background information in a model of classroom competence. In the first 70 years of educational research most of the school and community variables listed in Figure 1 were ignored "partly because they are too complex to study easily and partly because they [were] presumed to be remote from the basic purpose of education" (Dunkin & Biddle, 1974, p. 37).

Although there are many researchers, practitioners, and members of the public[1] who continue to agree with Dunkin and Biddle's early 1970's definition of pupil formative experiences, pupil properties, school and community contexts, and classroom contexts, as the conditions to which the teacher can do very little and must therefore adjust to (p. 41), court decisions such as Ann Arbor (Whiteman, 1980) and Lau v. Nichols (Pousada, 1979) have attempted to stimulate ways to prove otherwise.

Several major problems facing realization of the hope of stimulating change in adults' belief that they can do very little about students' formative experiences and pupil properties were recently described in the *Annual Report of the Social Science Research Council* (1980):

"In claiming a creative role for social science in the [legislative and educational] policy process, we must be candid about the limitations, emphasizing that no single study can answer the full range of questions that [are of concern.]" (p. xxii)

Yet it is believed that there are impressive reasons for asserting the usefulness of the social sciences in stimulating change in adults' belief about their influence on students' formative experiences and communicative properties. As demonstrated in the following review of past and current work in the development of competence, the social sciences continue to extend the observational powers of society and to compel "us to think in new ways about our own institutions, as well as our . . . potentials" (Annual Report, 1980, p. xvii).

Extending the observational system

Over two decades ago, Dell Hymes (1967) described the unmet need for a general theory and a body of knowledge within which aspects of the phenomenon of bilingualism could be properly assessed. He suggested two reasons why an aspect of all conversational styles such as diversity of code-switching had not received focused attention. First, those social scientists who had been asking the right sort of functional questions were not trained in ways of dealing with the linguistic face of the problem. Second, educators had not considered using a variety of ethnographic methods as a way of knowing the integrity of the message as an act, and the use of language in social life:

"In short [Hymes argued] that there must be a study of speaking . . . whose aim is to describe the communicative competence that enables a member of the community to know when to speak and when to remain silent, which code to use, when, where and to whom" (p. 13).

Exactly ten years after Hymes addressed the subject of bilingualism and the construct of communicative competence, McCormack (1976) observed that:

"previous study of language acquisition by monolingual children has been extended by substantial study of bilingual language acquisition. . . . Evidently, humans communicate in terms of complex processes such as mixing and code-switching among forms of both verbal and non-verbal behavior, and moreover, do what they do in a given case in response to [their perceptions and influences about the] social and cultural context of the communicative act. The complexity is observably there [but] is not presently reducible . . . to simple variations of "performance" on some universal base (p. 4). . . . [What we do now know however is that] by the age of about 22½ to 24 months the child has learned how to mean, in the sense that he has mastered the adult linguistic system, and thereafter he can and does use language to share meanings and participate." (p. 6)

Thus it has been recognized that despite the need for a convincing scheme for ordering one's thoughts about social growth, it is difficult to develop a tool that can assess the child's progress and, at the same time, take into account the speech or non-talk requirements of different contexts (Staub, 1978).

As many researchers who have followed the pioneering classroom and community discourse analysis and social group analysis work of John Gumperz (1972) and Susan Philips (1972) have confirmed, a child's capacity to interact with others cannot be validly assessed unless educators have a method for assessing their relationships across many domains: the family, the peer group, the community, and the school.

This means that researchers and practitioners who are trying to develop specific measures of social development from the knowledge base of 1981 have a problem solving situation. It would seem there are ways to begin to generate potential solutions from current knowledge base on pupils formative experience and pupil properties. A sample method for framing discussions of assessment will be described in the following elaboration of 3 synthesis tables. It should be pointed out that the content presented in the three tables is a selected and admittedly small pre-selected part of the current knowledge based on pupil's formative experience and pupil properties. Table 1 is a synthesis list of social skills that were extracted from the narrative of an article that was written to try to persuade child development and educational professors to teach practitioners more about ways of "seeing" social skills development.

Cartledge & Milburn (1978) tried to build a case for assessing whether any of the social skill demands listed in Table 1 are in fact operating in classroom domains in the following way:

"The goals to be reached in the academic curriculum are usually clear, but along with the acquisition of intellectual skills, there is another, mostly unarticulated 'hidden' curriculum that has to do with school behaviors, attitudes, and values" (p. 134)

Throughout the remaining sections of their twenty plus page argument the authors scatter various references to social behavior. The 21 prosocial behavior demands listed in Table 1 are assumed by Cartledge & Milburn to be related to school success, and hence, in their opinion can be used as a knowledge base for answering assessment questions such as:

What is the fit (and misfit) between abilities and settings . . . where is an ability frustrated for lack of a setting, or a setting unanswered for lack of an ability? (cf. Hymes, 1979, p. 16)

The objective of creating and reproducing a list of social skills such as Table 1 is to begin to synthesize the types of demands that have been identified in classroom domains. The objective of Table 2 as described by the authors, Greenberger & Sorensen (1974), is to develop a concept of youth and adolescence psychosocial maturity that recognizes that:

"In different [domains], the optimum balance among the capacities for self-maintenance, interpersonal effectiveness, and enhancement of social cohesion differ — that is, different 'amounts' of adequacy will be required of individuals in these areas of functioning." (p. 341)

TABLE 1 *prosocial behavior demands related to school success*

Make eye contact
Ask for extra help
Make positive comments to the teacher
Sit up straight
Nod in agreement as the teacher speaks
Come to class early
Ask for extra assignments
Seek out the teacher
Initiate contacts about work assignments
Smile at the teacher
Answer or try to answer questions
Use your body to show attention
Use your body to show persistence to tasks
Use your body, or face to show self-control
Show compliance with teacher demands
Follow directions
Show helping or sharing behavior as defined by school
Speak positively to others
Use your body to show control of aggression
Speak positively about academic materials
Remain on tasks

Despite the above qualification the authors still propose that some minimum of performance on the psychosocial dimensions they have identified from past research is expected across age and grade levels. The value they see in a list such as Table 2 is that each age related version of a scale based on these characteristics "will require validation against some external criterion of the trait in question." (p. 352) Therefore they suggest that a list such as Table 2 can serve as a tool. Researchers, practitioners, and other interested individuals, can begin to use the items in order to develop the external criteria which will be used to assess each trait at different ages. Although some recognition is given to the large amount of work this involves, the developers limit their discussion to the following argument:

"One would not expect self reliance to be expressed in the same way [by all children.] . . . change in the content of an assessment device [can take place] from time to time across all age groups. This periodic updating is required by the occurrence of social changes that might make once useful items poor indicators of [psycho-social maturity.]" (p. 352)

The creators of the psychosocial maturity assessment instrument

TABLE 2 *A model of psychosocial maturity*

Individual adequacy
Self-reliance
Absence of excessive need for social validation
Sense of control
Initiative

Identity
Clarity of self-concept
Consideration of life goals
Self-esteem
Internalized values

Work orientation
Standards of competence
Pleasure in work
General work skills

Interpersonal adequacy
Communication skills
Ability to encode messages
Ability to decode messages
Empathy

Enlightened trust
Rational dependence
Rejection of simplistic views of human nature
Awareness of constraints on trustworthiness

Knowledge of major roles
Role-appropriate behavior
Management of role conflict

Social adequacy
Social commitment
Feelings of community
Willingness to work for social goals
Readiness to form alliances
Interest in long-term social goals

Openness to sociopolitical change
General openness to change
Recognition of costs of status quo
Recognition of costs of change

Tolerance of individual and cultural differences
Willingness to interact with people who differ from the norm
Sensitivity to rights of people who differ from the norm
Awareness of costs and benefits of tolerance

(Greenberger & Sorensen, 1974)

admit that much work remains in developing items in each of the behavior and/or attitude categories listed in Table 2. Yet the assessment as it is presented in this paper provides a clearer understanding of the list of social prosocial demands in Table 1. By themselves the demands may be interpreted by the reader as hypocritical communicative competencies. However, as Greenberger & Sorensen point out, somehow adults as well as many pupils have learned that the enactment of behaviors or skills such as those outlined in Table 1 provide a means for accomplishing an end result such as the judgement of mature or competent. In their view asking questions about pupils' ability to deal with discrepancies, and pupils' ability to be aware of costs of the status quo work orientation is simply another way of asking:

> What are the meanings and values associated with the use of language in different sectors of professional groups in our society? (cf. Hymes, 1979, p. 16)

The authors of the review and theoretical articles on which Table 1 and 2 are based do not address how the social skills they have identified for the classroom and domain can be matched against some external criteria of communicative competence. Yet these lists do make a contribution. Taken as a whole the presentation of these variables strengthens the premise that the classroom and the wider social milieu cannot be ignored in any assessment of behavior. The lists remind educators to look for the possibility of behavior-environment interaction in searching for causes of competence. To make the leap from the need to consider the environment to selecting a standard for judging communicative behavior as-it-develops-in-context is, however, quite another matter. Recognizing the need to consider environment and social expectations about appropriate behavior indicates only where to search for parts to include in a model. While sound search strategies can shed light, the major problem in this diffuse literature arises in relating how classroom behavior demands and maturity behavior demands effect social development. Yet there may be a way to address this problem. The list presented in Table 3 is a synthesis of linguistic and ethnographic research findings on dimensions of communicative competence that can be observed and analyzed. The purpose of presenting this list along with Table 1 and Table 2 is to provide a tool for asking:

> What are the meanings and values associated with the use of nonverbal and verbal language in different age groups? (cf. Hymes, 1979, p. 16)

What comparable types of nonverbal and verbal competencies are recognized and used by children, youth, and adults as they enact the communicative participation demands listed in Table 3?

TABLE 3 *What comparable types of demands can we "see" in instructional settings and conversational settings*

— ways of entering and leaving
— ways to signal who has the right or obligation to make sense of what is going on
— styles of non-verbal behavior appropriate to the social setting
— social relations among speakers
— expectations of each speaker regarding what will occur
— an arrangement of tangible objects and rules for their use
— spatial distance between speakers
— ways to signal that you are following what is going on
— signals for who has the right to change the topic, or to speak more, or to stop speaking
— styles of communicative behavior appropriate to the content (e.g. gaze, pitch, intonation)
— ways to communicate that an individual has made an error, or that you need help, or attention
— ways to communicate information in abstract terms (e.g. moving from oral tradition or subjective content that is appropriate for some topics to a literate mode, or to the use of objective and abstract language)

The unanswered problem for future work in understanding communicative competence is how the work will from the 3 fields represented in Table 1, 2, and 3 be merged in teacher training. It is difficult to predict how useful these lists of classroom demands, psycho-social maturity demands, and communicative participation demands will be in helping researchers, practitioners, teachers and parents extend their skills in observing how children learn to deal with the social and personality display demands in our society and in our classrooms. Less uncertain, the lists can provide a way of stimulating thinking and discussions about children's capabilities in meeting these demands.

Thinking in new ways about children's potentials

In a 1971 review of the state of research in the field of human interaction, John Lofland made some remarks which aptly capture problems that remain in the study of communicative competence, that is, language used in order to share meanings and participate. Lofland pointed out that, as simple as it may seem, all social inquiry and social development theory reduce basically to the attempt to find answers to three questions:

1. What are the *characteristics* of a social phenomenon, the forms it assumes, the variations it displays?
2. What are the *causes* of a social phenomenon, the forms it assumes, the variations it displays?
3. What are the *consequences* of a social phenomenon, the forms it assumes, the variations it displays?

In offering advice to readers who are interested in actually observing or analyzing the characteristics of a social setting, Lofland began by pointing out that the vague term "social phenomenon" can be translated into at least six specific categories. Instead of asking "What are the characteristics of a social phenomena such as communicative competence?", one can try to adopt the point of view of the individual child as he or she moves out into the world. The image to keep in mind is that of child as strategist, maneuvering among other strategists. For the purpose of assessment the other strategists can "be taken as simply given and treated only as posing the problems to which the [child] as a strategist must respond." (p. 16)

Lofland would probably argue that the following expansion of his idea would not be the most valid method since we have not explicitly adopted "as the concepts of analysis the linguistic terms used by children themselves in designing their own acts" (p. 16). However, the aim of the following section is to provide a tool for those who are interested in building new meaning for Dunkin & Biddle's model of school and community contexts and pupils' skills. Since it is now known that the range and scope of social functions of language (Pinnell, 1975; Ritti, 1978) and the dimensions of interactional competence (Black, 1979) differ from bilingual classroom to bilingual classroom (Cazden, 1979) and from home to school (Cook-Gumperz, 1979; Florio & Shultz, 1979; Heath, 1982; Scollon & Scollon, 1982), the following images can serve as a reminder of the implications of ongoing research on social skills, psychosocial maturity and communicative competence. Each image is essentially a reminder of characteristics of communicative competence that have been identified by the researchers who are cited above. Each image is also a reminder of Hymes' (1967) call for the identification and description of communicative competence and his statement of the need "to show sociologists, linguists, enthnographers and others a way to *see* data as the interaction of language and social settings." (p. 13).

Images of relationships between individual development and development of communicative competence

As noted in earlier sections of this paper, the image of lifelong learning and the phenomenon of language socialization as a dual process is often blurred by bits of information.

"If each bit of information was like a 'yes' or 'no' answer in a twenty questions game, life might have the excitement of following the clues of a detective story. But [often] bits don't add up, each new fact is unrelated to the proceeding — that is the character of information today.
We can see this in education. . . . The average instructor teaches as much as he can of his own subject without the faintest idea of how it all adds up in the student's mind with the other subjects he [will be] taking" (Klapp, 1978, pp. 70–71).

The image of bits that don't add up suggests that there are some major definition problems with the presage and context variables that are included in Dunkin & Biddle's model for the study of classroom teaching. Deborah Tannen's (1979) work suggests that the term teaching skill needs to be reconsidered in light of the finding that perfect communication is an unrealistic image. In other words, an image of teaching as a dual process sociolinguistic skill raises the unanswered question of whether the incorporation of this meaning of skill into the Dunkin & Biddle illustrative model would involve an additional burden of demands on teachers. Consider the following dimensions of dual process sociolinguistic skill:

(a) ability to probe for bits of evidence that signal miscommunication;
(b) ability to hear and see metalinguistic signs, or contextualization cues which indicate how a speaker expects his words to be interpreted;
(c) ability to observe and document how these cues may vary with age, communicative development experience, and an individual's linguistic repertoire.

Gumperz' (1976) research on language and communication is helpful in addressing unanswered demand questions regarding dual process skill. The image conveyed by Gumperz is that an adult continually searches for contextual cues at three levels or channels of communication. A view of skill in light of Gumperz work would be that a dual process skill is universal rather than specific to a primary caretaker or teacher. Dual process skill in Gumperz view would include:

(a) nonverbal signals such as gaze direction, proxemic distance, kinesic rhythm or timing of body motion and gestures,

(b) paralinguistic signals: voice, pitch and rhythm,
(c) implicit semantic content of messages (p. 5).

The point Gumperz has made is that a systematic schedule of observation at this micro level can lead to construction of indices which would serve to help identify instances of interactional asymmetry or "uncomfortable moments" that can arise in any conversation. Equally as important Gumperz' work points out that:

"what is involved in cultural confusion and misunderstanding of communication is much more than the gross factors of racial or ethnic sterotypes and prejudices. Mere differences in values or attitudes are not the only causes. A large proportion of misunderstandings are traceable" (p. 2) . . .

to the judgement one speaker makes about the melodic patterns and kinesic patterns of the other. Consider again the list of social skills in Table 1. Somehow some children have learned that teachers could infer that someone is paying attention, or is mature and responsible, if they display certain mixes of nonverbal and verbal cues. Although sufficient information cannot always be elicited from subjects to prove whether school age children are aware of the symbolic and social meaning of contextualization cues that they use (— such as kinesic shifts, parakinesic shifts, proxemic shifts, modality shifts, audience shifts, register shifts, stance indicating shifts, and participant structure shifts—),[2] the argument Gumperz makes is that:

"there is reason to believe that the choice of communication strategy at the level of contextualization cues may be an important cause of miscommunication in public [settings]. Unlike casual meetings in the street, these events are governed by strict rules of procedure. They constitute instances of enforced contact where all participants know — or are assumed to know — the broad outlines of the formal rules and the parameters of the occasion" (pp. 11–12).

The theoretical notion of a relationship between communicative competence and contextualization cues is not a notion easily applied to unanswered questions regarding assessment. However, as shown in the following outline in Table 4, the notion that children and youth are capable of making inferences about others' nonverbal and verbal cues and are capable of signalling nonverbal and verbal cues that others can read has been demonstrated. The as yet unsolved problem to keep in mind as when reading the following list of new images of the characteristics of children's communicative competence is whether or not the category labelled "image" and the content included next to the category called "research support" can help to extend or modify the meaning of the variables that were presented in the model in Figure 1.

Thinking in new ways about context, classroom processes and pupil growth

As reflected in the outline presented above, one of the most significant features of the notion of communicative competence is the fact that it deals with how individuals convey social information about the situation they perceive is being constructed at the moment. Another aspect considers how the individual acts under the assumption that the other person shares the same expectations (or frames) about what is being said and what context they are building. Given these notions the unfinished task for this paper is to develop a clear image of: (a) how communicative competence research tries to assess the processes of classroom interaction, and (b) how communicative competence research tries to examine the extent to which children develop the ability to combine their own communicative competence rules with classroom interaction rules for participating along with the ability to display their academic knowledge.

In order to build this image of classroom research the remaining sections will address the process and product dimensions of Dunkin & Biddle's 1974 model for the study of classroom teaching. This task will be accomplished by presenting an overview of a small sample of recent studies of teaching which addressed the complex task of describing classroom interaction, and by discussing one study which related these processes to observable long range changes in pupil learning and performance.

Relationships among processes

The question of what students need to know in order to participate effectively in the classroom has been addressed by researchers who have attempted to broaden the concept of academic and social competence in order to encompass the functional aspects of language:

"The functional aspects of language concern effective language use in different social situations. It includes the speaker's-hearer's ability to accomplish tasks with language, the ability to communicate and interpret intentions, knowledge of the functions that language can

TABLE 4 *New images of children and Youth's communicative competence*

Image:	Child as persuader (cf. Cook-Gumperz, 1981)
Research Support:	The individual's use of multiple nonverbal and paralinguistic information cues in gaining adult attention can be measured. (Following Snow, 1979)
Image:	Child as adapter (cf. Corsaro, 1981)
Research Support:	The individual is capable of recognizing multiple sources of information including different social participation demands, distancing behavior demands, facial display demands, and turn yielding demands. Individual development along these dimensions can be measured. (Following Ekman, 1972)
Image:	Child as spontaneous apprentice (cf. Miller, 1977)
Research Support:	The individual's ability to produce a variety of hypotheses (theories, schemes, or frames) about how something will be said or could be said can be elicited and described. (Following Cazden, 1972)
Image:	Child as craftsman (cf. Feldman, 1976)
Research Support:	The individual can not only identify the linguistic meaning of speech acts performed by others, but can also accept the burden of identifying the social frame and discriminating clearly between relevant and irrelevant utterances. (Following McKay, 1974; Dore, 1980)
Image:	Child as social participant (cf. Philips, 1972)
Research Support:	The individual's knowledge of relations *between* people can be measured, e.g. are people strangers, or friends, or closely related. (Following Youniss, 1975)
Image:	Child as practical reasoner (cf. Cook-Gumperz, 1975)
Research Support:	The individual is aware of the notion that changes in behavior are demanded by different kinds of context. This awareness can be measured. (Following Parke, 1976)
Image:	Child as style shifter (cf. Labov, 1972)
Research Support:	The individual has a range of skills in showing how he or she can accomplish style shifting of some linguistic variables as the topic and social context change. Some of these skills of style shifting can be detected qualitatively in the minor self corrections of the speaker. Evidence from past studies point to age related differences in the development of this dimension of communicative competence. (Following Labov, 1972)
Image:	Child as ethnographer (cf. Mishler, 1972; 1979)
Research Support:	The individual student as linguistic ethnographer can display a range of awareness levels to changes in linguistic context and to the social identity of the speaker. As peer tutors children can specify what a stranger would have to know to perform any role in the classroom society. (Following Cazden, 1979; Mishler, 1978)
Image:	Child as negotiator (cf. Gumperz, 1976)
Research Support:	The consequences of an individual's use of multiple combinations of contextualization cues in attempting to influence a gatekeeper's decision, or a teacher's performance assessment can be identified. (Following Mehan, 1974; Erickson, 1975)

Image: Child as attention holder (cf. Sacks, 1972)
Research Support: The individual can learn what terms, fine details, and/or possible descriptions can best serve as an interesting and attention holding topic of conversation. The rules seem to be: first, learn what you are and what activities are appropriate to what you are (e.g. The baby cried. The mommy picked it up. She went to sleep.); second, learn what society expects you to be and what activities others expect of someone to whom terms refer (e.g. Sugar and spice and everything nice . . . that's what little girls are made of). The child's learning of social categories, or membership categories which are deemed important by the adult social community in which he or she lives and the activities commonly associated with these social categories are visible in the linguistic categories used across settings. (Following Garnica, 1979)

serve, the strategies of language that can be used to accomplish each function, and knowledge of the constraints that social situations impose on repertoire selection" (Mehan, 1980, p. 132)

Researchers such as Pinnell (1975), Ritti (1978), Black (1979), and Borman (1979) have addressed the task of identifying and assessing functions of language in the classroom. Building on work of language theorists such as Michael Halliday, Vera John, and Aaron Cicourel, these researchers have "provided clear pictures of differences in classroom conversational life" (Borman, 1979, p. 89) in preschool, kindergarten, first, second, fourth, and sixth grade classrooms. The major implications for oral language evaluation procedures from these studies is that it would not be appropriate to try to assess all of the functions listed in Table 5 in all classrooms situations. For example, Pinnell reported that over a period of 4 months, or 36 hours of tape-recorded talk of 12 children in 3 inner city classrooms over a period of 4 months, the instructional and social development task objectives of the classroom were geared toward practicing cooperation:

"The children used language to build social relationships, to offer suggestions to each other, to work out ways to share materials, to seek and give support, to establish friendship, and to invite others to join play or work activities. . . . As they worked together in the 'centers' or workshop areas of the classrooms, the students were often required to share materials and to work together. They turned to each other for advice and help. Sometimes they had to resolve conflict over property or territory." (p. 322)

Pinnell's finding that task situations in the classrooms that she studied could be described according to different quantitative breakdowns, or percentages of language functions,[3] was supported in Borman's (1979) 6 week, or 15½ hours of observational study of functions of language in reading groups, math groups, and tablework groups in two classrooms.

Continuing the tradition of studying competence through sociometric techniques such as paper and pencil tests, child developmentalists such as Ritti (1978) have found quantitative differences in the social message preferences of 240 second, fourth, and sixth graders. Ritti recently reported the results of tabulation of children's choice of one out of ten possible messages that might be said in a school test situation to another child. She argued that the differences in communicative choices that she found between the younger and older children offered support for the view that communicative competence develops as social competence does, with children becoming aware of functions such as those outlined in Table 5, and then, to some degree, accepting the values of the middle-class community where the unnamed school was located.

A study reported by Janet Black in 1979 attempted to convince other researchers and practioners that techniques of analysis such as Gay Pinnell's and Alyce Ritti's categorization of functions of language and Kathryn Borman's categorization of conversational groupings as shown in Table 5, could be readily applied to assessment of emerging behavior and development. The interactional competency checklist developed by Janet Black was based upon the following criteria:

1. the view that, since oral language develops, is practiced, and is utilized in the social or interactive context, teachers need help with finding ways to document behavior in a variety of classroom situations over an extended period of time
2. the view that observation of students' interactions with each other will provide the means of documenting the properties of interactional competence and academic competence listed in Table 6:

TABLE 5 *Multiple definitions of the functions of language*

A. Pinnell, G. S. (1975), Language in Primary Grades
    Instrumental language: "I want," or "I need."
    Language is used to satisfy needs or desires.
    Very often it takes the form of a request.
    Regulatory language: "Do this," or "Stop it!"
    Language is used to control the behavior of
    other people.

Interactional language: "Let's play," or "You and me."
The speaker uses language to establish and define
social relationships and to participate in the
"give and take" of social intercourse.
Personal language: "Here I am!"
Language is used to express one's individuality or
to give personal opinions and feelings.
Imaginative language: "Let's pretend."
The speaker uses language to express fantasies or
to create an imaginary world.
Heuristic language: "I wonder why?"
The speaker uses language to find out about things,
to ask questions, to seek information.
Informative language: "I've got something to tell you."
Language is used by a speaker to give information
about the world he or she has experienced.

B. Ritti, A. R. (1978), Social Functions of Children's Speech
Information: includes messages that are objective statements about the self, report facts, identify, classify,
analyze, and explain, e.g. "My paper is all done."
Directives: includes direct relational messages, including
regulative statements, demands, prohibitions, requests,
invitations, permission, and some suggestions, e.g.
"Don't look at my test."
Inductives: includes indirect relational messages that
reveal inner physical or psychological states,
physical sensations, emotional dispositions, needs,
hopes, wishes, likes, and dislikes, e.g. "I hope
you didn't cheat."
Evaluations: includes direct relational messages that
are essentially value statements such as evaluations,
appraisals, statements of obligations, inferences
about the listener, and some predictions, e.g. "Yours
is the good one."
Expressives: includes quasi-relational messages; they may
or may not affect the listener while they discharge
tension and emotion, e.g. "Wow!"

C. Borman, K. M. (1979), Children's Situational Competence
Regulative conversation groupings: the primary thrust
of the interaction is toward formulating rules,
negotiating about their enforcement, and regulating
the behavior (ongoing and future) of the participants.
Instructional conversation groupings: the primary thrust
of the interaction is toward the "school" learning
of the participants in the interaction and centers
on construction or reconstruction of knowledge.
Interpersonal conversation groupings: the primary thrust
of the interaction is either toward the development
of individual identity and differentiation from the
group or toward the development of interpersonal
skills and abilities (including "good manners").
Innovative-imaginative-expressive conservation groupings:
the primary thrust of the interaction is toward
spontaneous or creative expression of feelings.

TABLE 6 *Properties of interactional competence and academic competence*

— ability to adapt to changes in the theme of a play, or story plot
— ability to use appropriate gestures; appropriate facial expressions; appropriate body movement; appropriate social intonation; appropriate stress
— ability to become familiar with normal constraints and conditions of language and communication including:
   repairs (corrects) oral language
   recycles (rephrases) oral language
   repeats oral language
   terminates an exchange
— ability to demonstrate linking past experiences with present or possible future informational events

(Black, J. K. 1979, Assessing Children's Communicative Competence)

Relationships between processes and products

An important unanswered question that has emerged from assessments of classroom language functions such as those reported above is whether or not children learn more in classrooms where they speak more. "It has been hypothesized that many of the school problems experienced by minority group children may be attributable to . . . lack of learning opportunities which speech production provides" (Au, 1980, p. 91)

Recent reports of attempts to create reading lesson participation structures that are consistent with community oral story traditions of students in one school in Hawaii (Au, 1980) point out that minor changes in the number of child speakers and the evaluative or corrective role of the teacher over a two year period in the primary grades can promote the academic achievement of young minority students (cf. Wallat & Green, 1982). For example children who were permitted to continue to use devices such as overlapping another's answer; receiving help from others; commenting on others' messages; or contradicting others' answers, continued to demonstrate significantly better achievement scores on standardized tests one year after they completed primary school at the Kamehameha Early Education Program (KEEP).

The implications of the KEEP primary grade program for furthering current understanding of communicative competence and academic competence were succinctly stated in the research report:

— In terms of the cognitive content of the lesson, the complexity of the social interaction permitted by the teacher probably serves to prom-

ote the occurrence of a greater number of . . . unit ideas in the lesson
(p. 111)
— The analysis is felt to be of particular interest because this reading
lesson is an example of a culturally appropriate context for learning,
one which is comfortable for the children, comfortable for the teacher
and also productive of academic achievement (p. 112)

Summarization of Dunkin & Biddle's Model

This section concludes with the KEEP process product analysis
because it serves to highlight the themes that have been introduced. First,
the KEEP program has begun to test the hypothesis that minority children
can be taught with methods that build on, rather than negate, the
communicative competence devices they have developed before formal
school began. Second, the KEEP program has begun to test the hypothesis
that communicative competence is a dual process, that is, both the teacher
and students can learn, through their interactions, the sets of rules each has
already developed before meeting for the first time. Over the course of the
school year both the teacher and students become aware of how different
instructional contexts may or may not accommodate all of the linguistic
devices and rules they have mastered before the particular school year
began. In sum, the KEEP program has acted on ways to operationalize the
social competence definition of development as a life long course in
learning "progressively more sharply attuned communication interaction"
(Smith, 1968) and the communicative competence perspective which posits
the teacher as an integral part of the child's competence and the child as an
integral part of the teacher's competence (Cicourel *et al.*, 1974).

APPENDIX A

Characteristics of Contextualization Cues Reported to Date
   (a) Observed behaviors used in the establishment and maintenance of
       conversation units can be observed with low inference (Green, 1977;
       Gumperz & Herasimchuk, 1973)
   (b) Observation of means to realization of messages can be accomplished
       without subjective interpretation of intent (i.e. reliability figures in dealing
       with stress, pitch, intonation, and toning have been mainly in the 0.90's
       and high 0.80's) (Duncan & Fiske, 1977).
   (c) Cues when considered in context provide clarification of the structural and
       functional aspects of a communicative process.
   (d) Contextuating cues that can inform researchers and participants of the
       specifics of communicative competence and are useful in identifying social
       contexts demands include:

kinesics shifts	— body movement cf. Birdwhistell, 1970; Kendon, 1975)
parakinesic shifts	— aspects of action related to style of movement (cf. Birdwhistell, 1970)
proxemic shifts	— changes in interpersonal distance between speakers (cf. Erickson & Schultz, 1977)
postural shifts	— changes in gaze direction and facial expression (cf. Scheflen, 1973)
prosodic shifts	— changes in melodic patterns, voice tone, and pitch (cf. Cook-Gumperz, 1977; Kendon, 1975)
sequential shifts	— changes in relationship among different speakers, action sequences and events, e.g. who speaks first, second, third (cf. Argyle, 1972; McDermott, 1976; Sacks, Schegloff & Jefferson, 1974)
modality shifts	— shift in method of doing or acting or shift in communicative signals that adults use to mark change of social function, e.g. movement, kinesic gesture, semantic routine during arrival and leave taking (cf. Cook-Gumperz & Gumperz, 1976)
situational shifts	— within instructional lessons activities shift from formal or instrumental purpose to less formal instrumental purpose and back again (cf. Erickson & Schultz, 1977)
participant structure shifts	— within lessons there are differing rules of appropriateness for getting the floor, and/or maintaining topical relevance (cf. Erickson & Schultz, 1977; Green & Wallat, 1979; Philips, 1972)
involvement shifts	— involvement, non-involvement, or side involvement are signalled via direction and range of eye focus, body alignment and positioning, i.e. amount of physical movement in relation to context norm, and absence of voicing (cf. Goffman, 1972; Philips, 1974)
audience shifts	— message may involve class as a whole or one individual at a time (cf. Hymes, 1974)
temporal shifts	— reference to context establishment may include events in the past, present, or future, i.e. tieing (cf. Cook-Gumperz & Corsaro, 1976)
stylistic shifts	— message spoken with raised pitch and loud voice or a call to attention shifts to message still in a loud but slow-rhythm and measured pace with dropped pitch, i.e. an announcement (cf. Cook-Gumperz & Gumperz, 1976)
illocutionary force shifts	— shift in style has the force of a nonverbal representative, i.e. conform to requirement, or the force of a conversational representative, i.e. conform with a verbal response (Searle, 1969)
register shifts	— shift from formal and careful Language Instruction Register such as — We'll have to locate a container for that insect, to less formal — Ugh, look at that bug, get rid of it. (cf. DeStafano & Rentel, 1975; Halliday, 1973)

stance indicating
shifts   — Stance indicating is heavily dependent on the speaker-
                              learner context for interpretation (Feldman, 1976:
                              Halliday, 1976; Mishler, 1972)

Notes

1. See Annual Gallup Polls on Public Attidues Towards Education. Bloomington, Indiana: Phi Delta Kappa.
2. A glossary of these contextualization cues as defined by multiple researchers is included in Appendix A.
3. Interactional functions = 50% of 36 hours recorded; Regulatory functions = 13% of recorded language; Informational functions = 15% of children's recorded language.

References

Annual Report: Social Science Research Council, 1980, New York: Social Science Research Council.

Argyle, M. 1972, *The psychology of interpersonal behavior.* Baltimore: Penguin.

Au, K. H. 1980, Participant structures in a reading lesson with Hawaiian children: Analysis of a culturally-appropriate instructional event. *Anthropology and Education Quarterly,* 11(2), 91–115.

Birdwhistell, R. L. 1970, *Kinesics and Context: Essays on body motion communication.* Philadelphia: University of Pennsylvania.

Black, J. K. 1979, Assessing kindergarten children's communicative competence. In O.K. Garnica & M. L. King (eds), *Language, children and society.* New York: Pergamon Press.

Bloom. L. 1978, Commentary. *The Quarterly Newsletter of the Laboratory of Comparative Human Cognition,* 2(1), 1–4. (Formerly The Quarterly Newsletter of the Institute for Comparative Human Development) W. S. Hall & M. Cole (eds), San Diego: Center for Human Information Processing, University of California, San Diego.

Borman, K. M. 1979, Children's situational competence: Two studies. In O.K. Garnica & M. L. King (eds), *Language, children and society.* New York: Pergamon Press.

Cartledge, G., & Milburn, J. 1978, The case for teaching social skills in the classroom: A review. *Review of Educational Research,* 48(1), 133–56.

Cazden, C. B. 1972, *Language in early childhood education.* Washington, D.C.: National Association for the Education of Young Children.

— 1979, Language in education: Variations in the teacher-talk register. In J. A. Alatis & G. R. Tucker (eds), *Thirtieth Annual Georgetown University Round Table on Language and Linguistics: Language in public life.* Washington, D.C.: Georgetwon University Press.

Cherry-Wilkinson, L. 1981, Analysis of teacher-student interaction: Expectations communicated by conversational structure. In J. Green & C. Wallat (eds),

Ethnography and language in educational settings. Norwood, New Jersey: Ablex.

Cicourel, A. V., Jennings, K. H., Jennings, S. H. M., Leiter, K. C. W., Mackay, R., & Mehan, H. 1974, *Language use and school performance.* New York: Academic Press.

Cook-Gumperz, J. 1975, The child as practical reasoner. In B. Blount & M. Sanchez (eds), *Sociocultural dimensions of language use.* New York: Academic Press.

— 1977, Situated instructions: Language socialization of school age children. In S. Ervin-Tripp & C. Mitchell-Kernan (eds), *Child discourse.* New York:. Academic Press.

— 1979, Communicating with young children in the home. *Theory into Practice,* 18(4), 207–12.

— 1981, Persuasive talk: The social organization of children's talk. In J. Green & C. Wallat (eds), *Ethnography and language in educational settings.* Norwood, New Jersey: Ablex.

Cook-Gumperz, J., & Corsaro, W. A. 1976, Socio-ecological constraints on children's communicative strategies: Context in children's speech. In J. Cook-Gumperz & J. Gumperz (eds), *Papers on language and context.* University of California, Berkeley: Language Behavior Research Laboratory. Working Paper # 46.

Cook-Gumperz, J., & Gumperz, J. 1976, Context in children's speech. In J. Cook-Gumperz & J. Gumperz (eds), *Papers on language and context.* University of California, Berkeley: Language Behavior Research Laboratory. Working Paper # 46.

Corsaro, W. A. 1981, Entering the child's world: Research strategies for field entry and data collection. In J. Green & C. Wallat (eds), *Ethnography and language in educational settings.* Norwood, New Jersey: Ablex.

De Stafano, J. S., & Rentel, V. M. 1975, Language variation: Perspectives for teachers. *Theory into Practice,* 14, 328–37.

Dore, J. 1980, *The pragmatics of conversational competence: Two models, a method and a radical hypothesis.* Unpublished manuscript, Baruch College and the Graduate Center, City University of New York.

Dreitzel, H. P. 1973, *Childhood and socialization.* New York: Macmillan.

Duncan, S., & Fiske, D. W. 1977, *Face-to-face interaction: Research, methods, and theory.* New York: Erlbaum Associates.

Dunkin, M. J., & Biddle, B. J. 1974, *The study of teaching.* New York: Holt, Rinehart & Winston.

Ekman, P. 1972, Universals and cultural differences in facial expressions of emotions. In J. K. Cole (ed.), *Nebraska Symposium on Motivation* (Vol. 19). Lincoln: University of Nebraska Press.

Erickson, F. 1975, Gatekeeping and the melting pot. *Harvard Educational Review,* 1975, 45(1), 44–70.

Erickson, F., & Schultz, J. 1977, When is a context? Some issues and methods in the analysis of social competence. *Quarterly Newsletter of the Institute for Comparative Human Development,* 1(2), 5–9.

Feldman, D. H. 1976, The child as craftsman. *Phi Delta Kappan,* 58(1), 143–49.

Feldman, C. F., & Wertsch, J. V. 1976, Context dependent properties of teacher's speech. *Youth and Society,* 7, 227–58.

Florio, S., & Shultz, J. 1979, Social competence at home and at school. *Theory into Practice*, 18(4), 234–44.

Foster, S., & Ritchey, W. L. 1979, Issues in the assessment of social competence in children. *Journal of Applied Behavior Analysis*, 12, 625–38.

Garnica, O. K. 1979, The boys have the muscles and the girls have the sexy legs: Adult-child speech and the use of generic person labels. In O. K. Garnica & M. L. King (eds), *Language, children and society*. New York: Pergamon Press.

Garnica, O. K., & King, M. L. (eds), 1979, *Language, children and society*. New York: Pergamon Press.

Goffman, E. 1972, *Interaction ritual: Essays on face-to-face behavior*. London: Allen Lane.

Green, J. 1977, *Pedagogical style differences as related to comprehension performance: Grades one through three*. Unpublished doctoral dissertation, University of California, Berkeley.

Green, J., & Wallat, C. 1979, What is an instructional context: An exploratory analysis of conversational shifts across time. In O. K. Garnica & M. L. King (eds), *Language, children and society*. New York: Pergamon Press.

— 1981, Mapping instructional conversations: A sociolinguistic ethnography. In J. Green & C. Wallat (eds), *Ethnography and language in educational settings*. Norwood, New Jersey: Ablex.

Greenberger, E., & Sorensen, A. B. 1974, Toward a concept of psychosocial maturity. *Journal of Youth and Adolescence*, 3(4), 329–58.

Gumperz, J. J. 1972, Sociolinguistics and communication in small groups. In J. B. Pride & J. Holmes (eds), *Sociolinguistics*. Baltimore, Md.: Penguin.

— 1976, Language, communication and public negotiation. In P. R. Sanday (ed.), *Anthropology and the public interest*. New York: Acadmic Press.

Gumperz, J., & Herasimchuk, E. 1973, The conversational analysis of social meaning: A study of classroom interaction. In R. Shuy (ed.), *Georgetown University monographs in language and linguistics* (Vol. 25). Washington, D.C.: Georgetown University Press.

Gumperz, J. J., & Tannen, D. 1979, Individual and social differences in language use. In C. F. Fillmore *et al.* (eds), *Individual differences in language ability and language behavior*. New York: Academic Press.

Halliday, M. A. K. 1973, Explorations in the functions of language. London: Edward Arnold.

— 1976, Learning to mean: Explorations in the development of language. North Holland: Eleesevier.

Heath, S. B. 1982, Questioning at home and at school: A comparative study. In G. Spindler (ed.), *Doing the ethnography of schooling: Educational anthropology in action*. New York: Holt, Rinehart, and Winston.

Hymes, D. 1967, Models of the interaction of language and social setting. *Journal of Social Issues*, 23(2), 8–28.

— 1979, Language in education: Forward to fundamentals. In O. K. Garnica & M. L. King (eds), *Language, children and society*. New York: Pergamon Press.

Kendon, A. 1975, Introduction. In A. Kendon, R. M. Harris & M. R. Key (eds), Organization of behavior in face-to-face interaction. The Hague: Mouton.

Klapp, O. E. 1978, *Opening and closing: Strategies of information adaptation in society*. Cambridge: Cambridge University Press.

Labov, W. 1972, *Sociolinguistic patterns*. Philadelphia: University of Pennsylvania Press.

Lofland, J. 1971, *Analyzing social settings*. Belmont, CA: Wadsworth Publishing Co.

McCormack, W. C. 1976, Introduction. In W. C. McCormack & S. A. Wurm (eds), *Language and man: Anthropological issues*. Chicago: Aldine (Mouton Pub.).

McDermott, R. 1976, Kids make sense: An ethnographic account of the interactional management of success and failure in one first grade classroom. Unpublished doctoral dissertation. Stanford University.

McKay, R. 1974, Standardized tests: Objective/objectified measures of "competence". In A. V. Cicourel *et al.* (eds), *Language use and school performance*. New York: Academic Press.

Mehan, H. 1974, Accomplishing classroom lessons. In A. V. Cicourel *et al.* (eds), *Language use and school performance*. New York: Academic Press.

— 1980, The competent student. *Anthropology and Education Quarterly*, 11(3), 131–52.

Miller, G. A. 1977, *Spontaneous apprentices: Children and language*. New York: Seabury Press.

Mishler, E. G. 1972, Implications of teacher strategies for language and cognition: Observations in first grade classrooms. In C. B. Cazden, V. P. John & D. Hymes (eds), *Functions of language in the classroom*. New York: Teachers College Press.

— 1978, Studies in dialogue and discourse: III. Utterance structure and utterance function in interrogative sequences. *Journal of Psycholinguistic Research*, 7, 279–305.

— 1979, Would you trade cookies for popcorn: Talk of trade among six-year-old children. In O. K. Garnica & M. L. King (eds), *Language, children and society*. New York: Pergamon Press.

Mitzel, H. E. 1960, Teacher effectiveness. In C. W. Harris (ed.), *Encyclopedia of educational research* (3rd ed.). New York: Macmillan.

Parke, R. D. 1976, Social cues, social control and ecological validity. *Merrill-Palmer Quarterly*, 22, 111–23.

Perret-Clermont, A. N. 1980, *Social interaction and cognitive development in children*. New York: Academic Press.

Philips, S. U. 1972, Acquisition of rules for appropriate speech usage. In C. B. Cazden, V. P. John & D. Hymes (eds), *Functions of language in the classroom* New York: Teachers College Press.

— 1974, *The invisible Indian culture: Communication in classroom and community on the Warm Springs Indian Reservation*. Unpublished doctoral dissertation, University of Pennsylvania.

Pinnell, G. S. 1975, Language in primary classrooms. *Theory into Practice*, 14(5), 318–27.

Pousada, A. 1979, Bilingual education in the U.S. *Journal of Communication*, 29(2), 84–92.

Ritti, A. R. 1978, Social functions of children's speech. *Journal of Communication*, 28(1), 36–44.

Sacks, H. 1972, On the analyzability of stories by children. In J. Gumperz &

D. Hymes (eds), *Directors in sociolinguistics.* New York: Holt, Rinehart & Winston.

Sacks, H., Schegloff, E. A., & Jefferson, G. 1974, A simplest systematics for the organization of turn taking for conversation. *Language, 50,* 696–735.

Scheflen, A. E. 1973, *Communicational structure: Analysis of psychotherapy transaction.* Bloomington: Indiana University Press.

Scollon, R., & Scollon, S. B. K. 1982, Cooking it up and boiling it down: Strategies in Athabaskan children's story retelling. In D. Tannen (ed.), *Spoken and written language.* Norwood, New Jersey: Ablex.

Searle, J. 1969, *Speech acts.* Cambridge: Cambridge University Press.

Smith, M. B. 1968, Competence and socialization. In J. A. Clausen (ed.), *Socialization and society.* Boston: Little, Brown & Co.

Snow, C. E. 1979, The role of social interaction in language acquisition. In W. A. Collins (ed.), *Children's language and communication: The 12th Annual Minnesota Symposia on Child Psychology.* Hillsdale, New Jersey: Erlbaum.

Staub, E. 1978, Predicting pro-social behavior: A model for specifying the nature of personality-situation interaction. In L. A. Pervin & M. Lewis (eds), *Perspectives in interactional psychology.* New York: Plenum.

Tannen, D. F. 1979, *Processes and consequences of conversational style.* Unpublished doctoral dissertation, University of California, Berkeley.

Wallat, C., & Green, J. 1979, Social rules and communicative contexts in kindergarten. *Theory into Practice, 18*(4), 274–84.

— 1982, Construction of social norms by teacher and children: The first year of school. In K. Borman (ed.), *Social life of children in a changing society.* Hillside, New Jersey: Erlbaum.

Whiteman, M. F. (ed.) 1980, *Reactions to Ann Arbor: Vernacular Black English and education.* Washington, D.C.: Center for Applied Linguistics.

Youniss, J. 1975, Another perspective on social cognition. In A. Pick (ed.), *Minnesota Symposia on Child Psychology* (Vol. 9). Minneapolis: University of Minnesota Press.

Some comments on the terminology of language testing

Lyle F. Bachman
University of Illinois
Urbana, Illinois

Adrian S. Palmer
University of Utah
Salt Lake City, Utah

Introduction

The term "communicative competence" has been widely used and in many different ways.[1] To some, it simply means the ability to get a message across, regardless of the linguistic accuracy of the language employed. To others, it means the social rules of language use. And to yet others, it refers to a set of abilities including knowledge of linguistic, sociolinguistic, and discourse rules.

Recent attempts to develop a model of communicative competence and valid tests of its components (Bachman & Palmer, 1982) have led many in the field to reconsider the terminology of language testing. The purpose of this paper is to present a description of three attempts to specify what language tests measure and to clarify the meanings of technical terms. One conclusion reached is that there can be no test of communicative competence *per se*. Another is that a clearer notion of what constitutes linguistic competence, communicative competence, language skill, linguistic performance, communicative performance, and measures of linguistic and communicative performance is possible if one adopts a measurement approach.

Testing approaches

The skill-component approach

A modified version of Carroll's (1961) four-skill, four component model of language proficiency is illustrated in Figure 1. In this model, it is hypothesized that four types of language knowledge (referred to by Carroll as aspects and by others as components) are employed in each of the four language skill areas. The first three components describe types of knowledge: knowledge of phonological and orthographic rules; knowledge of (grammatical) structures; knowledge of the rules relating vocabulary items to their referents and, perhaps, the rules classifying these vocabulary items with respect to the sorts of grammatical structures in which they may be used. The fourth component, rate and general fluency, concerns the speed and ease with which the language user can employ the three types of knowledge — an ability one would expect to be influenced by the particular skill in which the rules are being used, as well as by other factors in the testing situation.

	Language Skills			
Components (Aspects)	Listening	Speaking	Reading	Writing
Phonology/orthography				
Structure				
Vocabulary				
Rate and general fluency				

FIGURE 1 *Language skills and their components*

The communicative approach

The communicative approach is one proposed by Canale & Swain (1980), and described by Canale (in this volume), and others (see the references in the paper by Canale in this volume). In the Canale/Swain framework, four areas of knowledge are proposed: Grammatical Competence, Sociolinguistic Competence, Discourse Competence, and Strategic Competence. These are characterized as follows: Grammatical Competence consists of knowledge of morphological rules, syntactic rules, vocabulary, (linguistic) semantic rules which determine the literal meanings of sentences, phonological rules which relate abstract linguistic categories to categories of positions and movements of the articulatory organs and to patterns of sounds, and orthographic rules which relate linguistic categories to shapes of letters, characters, the spelling of words, and so forth. Grammatical Competence, therefore, includes the first three *components* of the skills-component framework.

Sociolinguistic Competence consists of knowledge of rules governing the production and interpretation of language in different sociolinguistic contexts, including control of rules of meaning (how a particular utterance is to be interpreted in a particular context) and rules of form (which forms are appropriate in a given context).

Discourse Competence consists of knowledge of rules needed to produce a unified text as opposed to sentences in isolation. These include rules of cohesion, which relate sentences and clauses to one another (via, for example, pro-forms, synonyms, transition words, and parallel structures), and rules of coherence, which dictate the order in which various kinds of information (e.g. generalizations and examples) are presented, and which dictate restrictions on the inclusions of information (it must be relevant, not self-contradictory, and so forth).

The final area of competence, Strategic Competence, consists of the mastery of verbal and non-verbal strategies, and includes the use of dictionaries, paraphrases, gestures, and so forth to compensate for lack of knowledge in the three competencies mentioned above, as well as strategies for dealing with performance limitations such as noisy conditions, limitations in the knowledge of the other participants in the communication, and so on.

In this framework, Sociolinguistic, Discourse, and Strategic Competence are added to the skills component model, and the three components of phonology, orthography, structure, and vocabulary are collapsed into one.

The measurement approach

A third approach is found in the extensions of classical measurement theory proposed by Campbell & Fiske (1959) and by Lord & Novick (1968). In this approach, a set of test scores is viewed as being influenced by the following:

    1.   the mental abilities, or traits of the subjects being tested;

2. the method used to obtain the measurements;
3. the specific, or idiosyncratic properties of a particular test; and
4. error.

While the communicative approach has expanded understanding of the nature of language and communication, the terminology has become imprecise. In order to clarify these concepts an interpretation of the Canale/Swain (1980) communicative approach within the general framework of measurement theory is proposed (Figure 2). This interpretation is consistent with an understanding of what language tests measure and constitutes a statement of what the authors believe to be a reasonable set of hypotheses about the nature of language ability. (A more extensive discussion of this framework is provided in Bachman & Palmer, forthcoming.)

The communicative approach: an interpretation

The nodes and branches of the tree in Figure 2 specify a set of factors[2] affecting test scores. The horizontal brackets under these nodes specify the combination of factors constituting various aspects of language ability.

Trait factors consist of various types of *knowledge* (tacit or overt). These are understood to be completely mental in nature and to involve language.

Modal factors consist of *physiological abilities* which are brought into play whenever language is used. Method factors consist of aspects of the *testing* situation which affect test scores. Specificity consists of a factor which is unique to a given test — a factor which contributes reliable variance to scores on a particular test, in addition to that which is accounted for by the previously named factors. Finally, error consists of non-reliable (random) variance.

Trait factors. Trait factors consist of one general and several specific factors. The general factor consists of that portion of language ability which affects all language tests. No position is taken here concerning the nature of the general factor or the degree to which it is language related. Oller has attempted to explain what might account for this factor, and the reader is referred to his article: *Language Testing Research* 1979–1980 (1981).

The specific trait factors are of three types: linguistic, discourse, and interactive. The *linguistic* factors consist of those competencies which account for the forms and meaning of individual sentences without consideration of the contexts in which they are used. *Discourse* factors

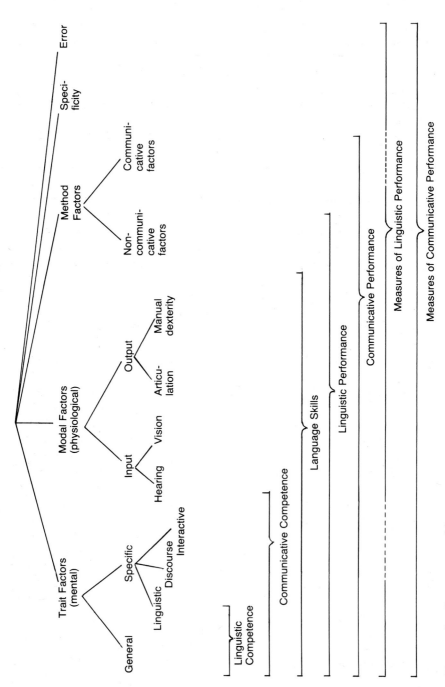

FIGURE 2 *Components of language test scores*

consist of those competencies — control of cohesion and coherence — which account for the combining of sentences to form discourse. The *interactive* factors are those competencies which account for the form and meaning of language used in contextualized, interpersonal communication: sociolinguistic and strategic competence.

Modal factors. Modal factors consist of physiological abilities which come into play whenever language is *used* in some way. These include control of the organs of speech production and reception. A language user might have linguistic knowledge of the rules of language representation but, due to physiological problems, be unable to employ these rules. For example, a language user might have acquired the knowledge of how abstract phonological units are represented in acoustic terms (format structure, noise components, transitions, timing, and so forth), yet, due to a loss of hearing ability, be unable to make use of this knowledge. Likewise, a language user's loss of fluency in pronouncing a language accurately after having been away from it from some time might be due, in part, to a loss of facility in *making* "known" articulatory movements. In the output mode, physiological abilities involve control of the muscles and organs of articulation (oral channel) and those of the hand (visual channel). In the input mode, they involve the functioning of the ears (oral channel) and eyes (visual channel).

Method Factors. Method factors come into play whenever language skills are *measured*. These consist of two types: The first involves testing factors which have nothing to do with the *communicative* use of language. They include: response type (multiple choice, fill-in-the-blank, etc.), the scorer (self, other, trained, untrained), and the procedures used (how the instructions are given, timing, and so forth). The second type of method factor consists of those aspects of *communicative* language use which are involved in the testing situation. Morrow (1977) describes seven features of communication which characterize communicative language from this perspective. First communication is interaction based; secondly, it involves unpredictability in both form and message; third, it varies according to sociolinguistic and discourse contexts; fourth it is carried out under performance limitations such as fatigue, memory constraints, and unfavorable environmental conditions; fifth, communication always has a purpose (i.e. to establish social relations, to express ideas and feelings, to persuade); sixth, it involves authentic, as opposed to textbook contrived language; and seventh, it is judged to be successful or unsuccessful on the basis of actual outcomes. Testing methods may involve all, some, or none of these features. The testing method is communicative to the extent that it involves interaction between the test taker and another language user. The more features of communication present in the testing situation, the more the test is a measure of communicative language use.

Specificity. Associated with any language test is some portion of reliable variance which is not explained by traits named in the researcher's theory. This variance is unique to a particular test and shared by no other. It is important not in what it is but in its magnitude. If it is large, little reliable variance remains to be explained via *named* factors.

Error. After all the reliable variance in a set of test scores has been accounted for, there will remain a portion of the variance which is random. As with specificity, this error variance is important in its magnitude. The greater the error component, the lower the reliability of the test.

The Terminology of Language Proficiency

Given the preceding account of sources of variance in test scores, more precise definitions of terms used to describe language proficiency can now be provided. The following terms will be defined: linguistic competence, communicative competence, language skill, linguistic performance, communicative performance, and measures of linguistic and communicative performance. Although a general trait factor is being included in the definitions, whether or not it should be a part of the competencies defined is still an open question.

Linguistic competence. Linguistic competence consists of that portion of test scores attributable to the mental abilities associated with the general trait factor and of the specific linguistic factors. It excludes the specific discourse and interactive factors, as well as, the modal, method, specificity, and error factors.

Communicative competence. Communicative competence consists of that portion of test scores attributable to the mental abilities associated with linguistic competence. In addition it includes discourse competence and the knowledge of interactive rules which account for the form and interpretation of language used in contextualized interpersonal situations. It excludes modal, method, specificity, and error factors.

Language skills. Language skills consist of that portion of test scores attributable to trait and modal factors but excluding method, specificity, and error factors. The broken portion of the bracket in Figure 2 indicates the omission of factors above it.

Linguistic performance. Linguistic performance consists of that portion of test scores attributable to the general and linguistic trait factors, the modal factors, and the non-communicative method factors. (This definition of linguistic performance includes method factors such as, for example, the ability to answer multiple-choice type questions. Since these are factors in linguistic performance, which apply only in testing situation, the definition of linguistic performance, as well as the terms which follow need to be modified if they are to be defined for more general application.)

Communicative performance. Communicative performance consists of that portion of test scores attributable to the trait factors, the modal factors, the non-communicative method factors, and the communicative method factors. A test score will be a "better" indicator of communicative performance to the extent that the test *method* involves more of the features of communication.

Measures of linguistic performance. Measures of linguistic performance include that portion of test scores attributable to the general and linguistic trait factors, the modal factors, the non-communicative method factors, specificity and error. The broken portion of the bracket in Figure 2 indicates the *omission* of factors above it.

Measures of communicative performance. Measures of communicative performance include that portion of test scores attributable to the trait and modal factors, the non-communicative method factors, the communicative method factors, specificity and error.

Test scores and factor scores. A *single* language test score must reflect at least general and linguistic trait factors, modal factors, non-communicative method factors, specificity, and error. It *can* also reflect discourse and interactive trait factors and communicative competence, a language skill, linguistic performance, or communicative performance. However, if one were to administer an extremely large number of tests at the same time (20 or more) to an extremely large number of subjects (1,000 or more), one might have enough information to arrive at a *factor score* for an individual which could be taken as a measure of linguistic competence *per se*, and so forth. Until this type of research has been done, it is suggested that the terms *score, measure,* and *test* be used with enough qualifying descriptions to specify the trait, modal, and method factors involved.

Communicative competence. The term communicative competence consists of the two words "communicative" and "competence." Combined, the two mean competence to communicate. The term competence goes back to Chomsky (and deSaussure). Chomsky (1965) used it to refer to "the speaker-hearer's knowledge of his language," and he distinguished it from performance, which is "the actual use of language in concrete situations." Competence, then, clearly refers to knowledge as separate from the ability to use this knowledge.

With the current interest in testing communication, it has become common to speak of tests of communicative competence without concern for the competence/performance distinction. This has, in turn, led to the erroneous notion that it is possible, by means of a *single* test, to assess any kind of competence desired. In addition, many educators and researchers have lost sight of the fact that communication involves two parties, and success in communicative performance will always be dependent upon the abilities of two people. Thus, in contrast to measures of linguistic performance, measures of communicative performance must not be taken as an indication of some absolute amount of success an individual has in communicating. An individual's success will always be dependent, to some extent, upon his or her audience.

Summary

The term *competence* should be reserved for strictly mental abilities. The term *skill* should be reserved for mental abilities plus physiological abilities. *Performance* should be reserved for language use in a given context. *Linguistic performance* should be reserved for language performance in a context marked for the *absence* of features defining a communicative situation. *Communicative performance* should be reserved for language performance in a context marked by the presence of features defining a communicative situation. *Measure* should be reserved for an actual test score, including the specificity and error components, and *test* should be reserved for an instrument used to obtain a measure, with all of the qualifications placed on the term *measure*.

Notes

1. We would like to thank Michael Canale for raising some of the issues we have dealt with in this paper. We would also like to thank Pat Mitchell for her many helpful comments and criticisms.
2. The term "factor" is used here in the non-technical sense of a contributory influence, and not necessarily in the technical sense of a latent variable in factor analysis.

References

Bachman, L. & Palmer, A. S. 1982, The construct validation of components of communicative proficiency. *TESOL Quarterly*, 16, 4, 449–65.

Bachman, L. F. & Palmer A. S. Forthcoming, *Basic Concerns in Language Test Validation*. Reading, Mass: Addison-Wesley.

Campbell, D. T., & Fiske, D. W. 1959, Convergent and discriminant validation by the multitrait-multimethod matrix. *Psychological Bulletin*, 56,(2).

Canale, M., & Swain, M. 1980, Theoretical bases of communicative approaches to second language teaching and testing. *Applied Linguistics*, 1(1), 1–47.

Carroll, J. B. 1961, Fundamental considerations in testing for English language proficiency of foreign students. *Testing the English proficiency of foreign students*. Washington, D.C.: Center for Applied Linguistics.

Chomsky, M. 1965, *Aspects of the theory of syntax*. Cambridge, Mass.: M.I.T. Press.

Lord, F. M., & Novick, M. R. 1968, *Statistical theories of mental test scores*. Reading, Mass.: Addison-Wesley.

Morrow, K. E. 1977, *Techniques of evaluation for a notional syllabus*. University of Reading: Centre for Applied Language Studies. (Study commissioned by the Royal Society of Arts, London.)

Oller, J. W., Jr. 1981, Language testing research (1979–1980). In R. Kaplan (ed.), *Annual revue of applied linguistics*, 124–50.

Some implications of communicative competence research for integrative proficiency testing

Richard P. Duran
Educational Testing Service

In a recent sketch on the evolution of language proficiency tests, Bernard Spolsky (1978) comments on the historical development of discrete-point proficiency tests and the subsequent emergence of other views of language proficiency assessment which were critical of the notion of discrete-point assessment. Two such views on language assessment — or communication assessment, speaking more broadly — are *integrative proficiency testing* and *research in the area of communicative competence.* As Spolsky (1978) and other reviewers of proficiency research note, views such as integrative proficiency testing of proficiency and communicative competence research stress a fundamental assumption that language skills are best evidenced and evaluated in contexts where language is used naturally. Within integrative testing and communicative competence research there are, of course, significant variations in how "natural" a context must be to serve as the medium within which to study communicative skills. Integrative approaches to proficiency testing stress the notion that linguistic skills need to be studied as they interact with each other in naturally occurring segments of language use, but the contexts for assessment may vary from formal testing contexts to elicitations of speech or writing in situations in everyday settings. Studies of communicative competence as evidenced in the research literature in ethnography of communication, sociolinguistics, and conversational analysis by and large couple analysis of naturally occurring speech with study of the interpersonal/interactive dynamics that arise in communicative contexts given their sociocultural constraints.

This paper will focus on a discussion of some implications of communicative competence research on use, interpretation and development of integrative proficiency tests. The central argument to be presented is that persons using integrative language proficiency tests may improve the interpretation and theoretical design of proficiency tests by attending to some of the discourse and interactional skills uncovered in communicative competence research. Two ways in which this can occur seem readily apparent. The first way stresses better appreciation of differences between the objectives of integrative proficiency testing and the methods and findings of communicative competence research. In particular, it is very important for users of existing language proficiency tests to be better informed about aspects of everyday discourse behavior that reference the notion of "communicative competence," but which may be difficult or impossible to study by means of integrative proficiency tests as they are presently known. Related to this point is the need for interpreters of language proficiency test performance to be sensitive to the potential influence of background factors and interactional competencies among language proficiency examinees which affect performance on proficiency tests.

A second apparent way in which to link communicative competence research findings to integrative proficiency tests, is to suggest experimental development and evaluation of new proficiency tests which assess skills along language proficiency dimensions identified through communicative competence research. In advocating this direction for test development, it will be made clear, in the course of this paper, that it is not sensible to use the terms "communicative competence tests" to describe new proficiency tests that might draw from findings of communicative competence research. The reason for this should become apparent in the course of the paper.

Before beginning the discussion of how to improve use and development of integrative proficiency tests, an overview of the meaning of "integrative proficiency testing" and "communicative competence research" will be presented.

Integrative proficiency testing

The general notion of "integrative proficiency tests" may be best understood by contrasting it with the idea of discrete-point proficiency tests. Discrete-point proficiency tests are composed of test items, each of which addresses an examinee's skill in controlling a single surface rule of language related to morphology, phonology, grammar or vocabulary. As a further constraint, discrete-point tests most often aim to assess control of particular surface rules in a standard variety of language in a single productive or receptive mode of language use. In effect, each modality of language use — speaking, writing, aural comprehension and reading is distinguished from other modes. Skills comprising language use in any modality are viewed independently of skills in any other modality (for a thorough discussion see e.g. Lado, 1961). This compartmentalization of language-use skill by modality and control of surface rules is often accompanied by an implicit or explicit assumption that language proficiency in a given modality is hierarchial in nature. High level skills such as, oral production of coherent sentences, are reliant on intermediate level skills of syntax and vocabulary choice and, in turn, these intermediate level skills are founded on more basic skills relating to phonology and morphology. A further common assumption of the discrete-point approach to proficiency testing is that the language skills tested are referenced by a standard variety of language whose structure and rules of formation determine absolutely the permissible variations language users may manifest in being judged proficient in a language.

The integrative view of language proficiency assessment contrasts with the discrete-point view in the assumption that proficiency is best assessed by looking at language use requiring coordination of a number of sub-skills of language use.

Examples of integrative proficiency tests include tests (or subtests) described as: (a) written dictation; (b) cloze procedure completion of sentences; (c) written composition; (d) oral interviews; (e) reading aloud; and (f) multiple choice tests of reading comprehension requiring inference (Oller & Perkins, 1980). Each of the kinds of tests or task categories mentioned requires examinees to process language in a complex way involving coordination of different surface rules of language, but may or may not, in general, require other sets of social or cognitive skills which are related to actual language use. Oral interviews, for example, rely on social interaction conventions shared among conversationalists.

Oller (1979) has introduced the notion of a *pragmatic proficiency test* as a more precise prescription of what *intergrative proficiency tests* are like when the issues of contextual relevance of language use are of concern in proficiency testing.

According to Oller a pragmatic test of proficiency is:

"any procedure or task that causes the learner to process sequences of elements in a language that conform to the normal contextual constraints of that language, and which requires the learner to relate sequences of linguistic elements via pragmatic mappings to extralinguistic context." (Oller. 1979, p.38)

tests, stresses use of language in a manner relevant to normal ways in which structures of language are coordinated in everyday communication, and excludes language tasks which are highly artificial. An example of this latter sort of task is rote recitation of sequences of materials without attention to meaning.

Pragmatic proficiency tests (as a variety of integrative proficiency tests with high face validity) have, according to Oller, two principal constraints. First, processing of language by examinees on pragmatic tests must be constrained temporally and sequentially in a way consistent with the real world occurrences of the language forms that happen to comprise test materials or speech in testing situations. This constraint could imply, for example, that encountering sentences on a reading comprehension test would require that an examinee would process such sentences as meaningful sentences, rather than as just strings of words with no communicative intent.

A second constraint proposed by Oller for the pragmatic variety of integrative proficiency testing is that such tests use language in a way resembling natural occurrences of language outside testing contexts or formal language testing environments. According to Oller, the meaning of language understood or produced in pragmatic tests must link somehow to a meaningful extralinguistic context familiar to the proficiency examinee.

Oller's (1979) development of the notion of pragmatic proficiency tests seems troublesome in that the naturalness criteria for language use on proficiency tests do not address well the artificiality of testing contexts in and of themselves, and how such artificiality constrains language use. Within the research field of proficiency test development, this issue is better addressed by the notion of *direct* versus *indirect* tests of language proficiency as forwarded, for example, by John Clark (1978).

Clark discusses direct assessment of language proficiency in terms of the natural use of language by examinees in the following fashion:

"From a theoretical standpoint the most direct procedure for determining an individual's proficiency in a given language would simply be to follow that individual surreptitiously over an extended period of time, observing and judging the adequacy of performance in the language-use areas in question: buying train tickets; ordering a meal; conferring with colleagues on work related matters; conversing with friends on topics of current interest; writing a note for the plumber; ordering business supplies by correspondence; and so forth. It is clearly impossible, or at least highly impractical, to administer a 'test' of this type in the usual language learning situation. Nonetheless, the development of proficiency measurement procedures that can properly be considered 'direct' must be based on approximating, to the greatest extent possible within the necessary constraints of testing time and facilities, the specific situations in which the proficiency is called upon in real life." (Clark, 1978, p. 23).

In passing, it might be noted that Clark's views of language use and proficiency assessment are not altogether unlike the views of communicative competence researchers interested in studying language use in natural contexts. Clark indicates that direct proficiency tests should model everyday language use situations, but he acknowledges that testing contexts can only approximate the real world.

Pragmatic proficiency tests in Oller's sense, require language use very often in artificial contexts, as might occur, for example, in filling in missing words on cloze test items, or in transcription of sentences or small stretches of discourse input through earphones accompanied by varying degrees of ambient electronic noise. Language use in pragmatic proficiency tests of this sort requires integration of language skills (and concomitant use of cognitive skills as well), but the "naturalness" of testing contexts is very limited, substantially decontextualized from the social and material world within which language is normally used.

Oller and his colleagues (see Oller, 1979; Oller & Perkins, 1980), and many others, argue that high intercorrelations among measures of pragmatic proficiency test performance show that language proficiency is a unitary skill. The argument is based on numerous and, at times, impressive, correlational studies which show substantial correlations between, for example, accuracy in dictation of oral speech and performance on other varieties of indirect proficiency tests, such as cloze tests and discrete-point test of skill in vocabulary, grammar or phonology.

Oller and others also point out that scores on pragmatic proficiency tests of the sort mentioned also tend to show correlations of high magnitude with scores on tests of general mental abilities and learning achievement. Oller suggests, in fact, that quite possibly, language use skill measured by pragmatic proficiency tests, and cognitive aptitudes in examinees measured by appropriate tests, identify one and the same repertoire of mental skills. The latter possibility in some ways resembles the notion of cognitive/academic language proficiency (CALP) (as opposed to Basic Interpersonal Communicative Skills [BICS]) recently put forward by Cummins (1980). It could be suggested, however, that BICS is just as cognitive as CALP, though decontextualized cognitive skills or genres of formal thought are more emphasized in CALP.

In concluding this overview of integrative proficiency testing, it should be emphasized that the approach of direct proficiency assessment is more likely to stress the use of language in naturalistic contexts than is indirect proficiency testing, which is of Oller's pragmatic variety. A second point is that the direct proficiency testing approach, while developed within the contexts of psychometric theory, seems to be open to development of new proficiency assessment techniques based on language use in natural contexts. In contrast, the indirect pragmatic or integrative view proposed and investigated by Oller and others would suggest that some pragmatic tests (with low face validity) are already adequate as assessment devices for language proficiency in general.

Communicative competence research

Communicative competence research has historically been developed independently from research in proficiency testing. What cross-fertilization has occurred stems largely from proficiency researchers interested in improving the content validity of proficiency tests. Historically, communicative competence research stems from sociologists', ethnographers', and cultural anthropologists' interest in language use and communication in everyday contexts. Communicative competence as defined in this paper entails the control of all the functions which language may serve in everyday sociocultural contexts (Gleason & Weintraub, 1978). While it is a simplification, the range of such functions as might be described "referential," "social" and "directive" (op. cit.). Referential functions designate speech acts which transmit meaningful information encoded in speech from a speaker to a listener. Social functions of speech refer to speech acts that go beyond conveyance of factual meaning to listeners to include information about social roles, relationships, and identities shared among speakers in a setting. Directive functions of speech refer to use of speech in commands and requests wherein what is said by one speaker to another is intended to motivate action or thought of a specific variety in a listener.

The distinctions between the three speech functions or general classes of speech acts mentioned are not separable in real world contexts since all three may occur simultaneously in speech. It is important to note, however, that the emphasis of communicative competence research is on the successful conduct of social or practical business in a setting and that control of surface rules of a language is not viewed from the same perspective adopted by language proficiency test researchers. In the communicative competence approach success in communication is viewed more in terms of a reciprocal contract of communicative cooperation (called the Cooperative Principle of Communication by Grice, 1975) for speaking shared among participants. In part, this contract is negotiated as people interact and evolve their interactional agenda in a setting.

Some of the most important and interesting issues for study in communicative competence research concern speakers' control of their discourse so that it reflects the social dynamics of interaction. Sociolinguists and conversational analysts study such control in terms of the discourse structure of utterances, and in terms of relationships that arise across utterances as speakers converse. Some examples adopted from a recent paper by Richards (1980) follow.

Adjacency pairs in discourse refer to the explicit coupling of successive utterances of speakers following conventions of speech use and perceptions of the social purpose of utterances.

Richards (1980) offers examples of this, such as the following:

Request for Information-Grant:	A.	"Do you have the time?"
	B.	"It's five o'clock."
Request-Grant:	A.	"May I have some coffee?"
	B.	"Sure, help yourself."
Complaint-Apology:	A.	"It's half past 6:00."
	B.	"Sorry I'm late."
Summons-Answer:	A.	"Jimmy!"
	B.	"Coming, Mother."

In each of the examples the impression is given that two conversationalists must be capable of recognizing an expected coupling between what one speaker says and what another might be expected to say immediately afterwards. This form of communicative competence is highly dependent on conversationalists' shared knowledge of an immediate communicative context and, as well, on what range of social role relationships are possible between speakers in a setting.

More generally, researchers in conversational analysis and communicative competence are interested in the broader organization of discourse in an interactional setting and how interlocutors take turns in speaking to each other. These are areas of language competence which enter only indirectly in assessments of language proficiency by means of existing tests. In informal social contexts, conversations which seem relatively unstructured reveal, when studied closely, global organizational constraints which require effective use of language by speakers. *Openings and closings* of conversation show recurrent use of formulaic-like language as occurs, for example, in extending greetings when persons meet again or in extending "goodbyes" when persons take leave from each other.

Some communicative activities which researchers in the area of communicative competence have studied are more tightly structured than conversations. One example is organization of speech in classrooms.

Mehan (1979) has studied turn-taking during oral recitation in classrooms and found that in many circumstances a network pattern of speech roles (Teacher Initiate, Student Reply, Teacher Evaluate) between teacher and student occur. While *adjacency pair* analysis might be used to study particular pairings of teacher-child speech acts, the Mehan analysis suggests that a teacher and child share a more global set of expectations about oral recitation as an activity.

Research in bilingual children's classroom communication by Carrasco, Vera & Cazden (1981) and Garcia & Carrasco (1981) suggests that the kind of event analysis provided by Mehan is highly dependent on the previous history and style of interaction, and roles within an interaction, shared among communicative participants. Specifically, Carrasco, Vera & Cazden found that a young bilingual school child was unable to communicate well about a language arts spelling task when queried by a teacher, but was observed to be able to teach the same language arts in question fluently to another child in a peer teaching activity.

A third form of discourse behavior investigated by researchers in communicative competence is *repairs* in conversation. According to Richards (1980), based on the work of Schegloff & Sacks (1973), the term "repair" refers to efforts by speakers to correct interactional trouble spots in conversation. Need for repairs occurs when a speaker is uncertain of what an earlier speaker said, disagrees with what another speaker has said, or when a speaker evidences some loss of fluency in speech. In the former case, a speaker attempting to undertake a conversational repair may utter to another interlocutor statements such as, for example, "What did you say?", or "Run that by me again." Some repairs may be of a character that reflects differences in points of view among speakers that require polite negotiation through further discussion as in "Gee, . . . I don't know . . ." or "Come on . . . you know better than that."

Loss of fluency as when a person slows rhythm of speech or hesitates in order to search for a best word are another example of conversational repairs.

Repairs in discourse seem to evidence speakers' ability to monitor interaction with other speaker's in a manner reflective of awareness of polite strategies by which to continue or terminate conversation. From the communicative competence research standpoint, ability to undertake repairs is always a positive indicator of communicative skill. In contrast, some forms of repair — such as coping with lack of fluency through circumlocution — might be viewed as negative indicators of language ability from a proficiency point of view.

Richards (1980), citing Tarone (1977), lists the following types of repairs, in addition to circumlocution, as common among second language learners: (a) approximation (as in "shop" for "department store"); (b) word coinage (as in "ice crushing" for "ice breaking"); (c) borrowing (as in code-switching due to unavailability of a word in the language of conversation); (d) mime (sounding the physical thing designated by a word which is unavailable); (e) topic shift (sudden transition away from a discussion due to lack of vocabulary in a topic domain); and (f) topic avoidance, also due to lack of vocabulary.

As with circumlocution, the other repair strategies mentioned when viewed from the vantage point of communicative competence research, indicate successful application of strategies to continue communication and interaction. From traditional approaches to proficiency testing, use of repair strategies may be taken on many occasions as an indication of lack of language proficiency, rather than as positive evidence of communicative skill.

One final area of communicative competence research to be discussed is analysis of the function of paralinguistic cues in speech. Such cues can involve controlled use of prosody (pace of speech), stress (manipulation of amplitude of speech), and intonation. Some of the research of John Gumperz and his colleagues (Gumperz & Kaltman, 1980; Collins & Michaels, 1980; Gumperz & Tannen, 1979; Bennett, 1980) has focused on how sounds in speech are grouped paralinguistically and how use of paralinguistic cues — termed contextualization cues in their work — help carry important parts of the message load in speech. Gumperz & Kaltman (1980) and Gumperz & Tannen (1979) in their work present and analyze many examples of speech by learners of English which reveal inappropriate use of contextualization cues leading to speech which native listeners of English can't understand, despite the fact that the speech is perfectly intelligible in terms of grammar, word choice, and semantic content.

A related set of issues concerning contextualization cues in speech has been the subject of investigation by Bennett (1980), Erikson (1980), and Scollon (1981), among others. These researchers in the sociolinguistics and ethnography of communication tradition have given attention to maintenance of rhythmicity in speech and to rhythmicity in use of so-called "back channel" cues, by which listeners acknowledge receipt of information from speakers. Research of this sort suggests that speakers establish and manipulate tempo in speech as a strategy to control an audience's attention and to establish evidence that there is cohesion in conversation. Lack of skill in manipulation of synchrony or rhythm in speech may lead to false starts in speaker's assumption of conversational turns, interruption of other's speech and to awkward, repeated use of repair strategies to keep the conversation continuing.

Implications of communicative competence research for integrative proficiency testing

As mentioned earlier, there are two immediate ways in which integrative proficiency testing — particularly direct proficiency testing — might benefit from findings of communicative competence research. First of all, there is a need for language proficiency test developers and test users to recognize important aspects of language use that are not addressed specifically in existing assessment methods, and to learn how such aspects of skilled language use contribute to communication.

In interpreting performance on existing proficiency tests, there is a need for language test users to be sensitive to ways in which control of the surface features of language might be confounded with interactional discourse skills. Formal language proficiency test contexts, as social contexts themselves, subsume language use within their social norms for interaction and, though their social norms are not the direct object of study, they may critically influence assessments of language proficiency.

While direct oral proficiency tests often elicit speech from examinees in naturalistic conversational settings, interpreters of examinees' speech need to be sensitive to interactional dynamics in speech elicitation which affect the speech samples collected. Users of direct proficiency tests (employing the *FSI oral interview test,* for example) (FSI, 1970) might be assisted in interpreting the validity of the technique by attention to the larger range of discourse skills which their examinees evidence. In an important sense, skills in communicative competence of the sort that have been reviewed in this paper are a prerequisite for sustaining speech in oral proficiency tests relying on an interview technique. An important issue in validating the extended content and construct validity of such direct proficiency tests involves investigation of how examinees' language varies as a function of examinees' characteristics, background, and discourse topic and other parameters of a speech event. This issue seems to be of particular importance in sensitively calibrating performance standards on oral proficiency tests for use in certification of examinees' professional qualifications, as for example in certification of bilingual school teachers' language proficiency. In this latter case it is essential that assessments of teachers' oral skills in two languages be accurately reflective of the types of skills germane to the conduct and management of classroom activities, and to the language background of students. Insensitive calibration of performance standards on oral proficiency tests for teachers can lead to serious misratings of teachers' communicative competence in classroom settings, especially in cases where teachers' background shows strong exposure to nonstandard dialects of English and nonstandard varieties of a non-English language.

A second way in which integrative proficiency tests might benefit from communicative competence research is by future development of new assessment procedures sensitive to social influences on discourse behavior. Language proficiency test developers who wish to develop scales of communicative competence skills are unlikely to leave their psychometric perspective — nor should one expect them to. Accordingly, the instrument development strategies for communicative competence skills should adhere to the highest standards of psychometric test design principles.

Rating of oral speech samples along dimensions of communicative competence that have been discussed in this paper, along the general outline of procedures followed in the *Foreign Service Institute Oral Interview Test* (FSI, 1970), might be an effective way to create broadbased proficiency tests. A detailed discussion of such a psychometric approach can be found in the work of John Clark on the ETS Common Yardstick measurement project and the work of Lyle Bachman and Adrian Palmer and Michael Canale & Merrill Swain (1979). These approaches all have in common a basis in psychometric theory and test development and an attempt to develop numerical scales of examinees' oral skills in communication that go beyond traditional concern for examinees' control of surface features of language.

In the space remaining, the possibility will be discussed of the development of new proficiency assessment techniques which, like integrative tests, require coordination across skills in language, but which also have substantial ecological validity in terms of social circumstances of language use. These are assessment techniques which are based on a primarily qualitative evaluation of interactional skills of an examinee in naturalistic or nearly naturalistic language use encounters. Such new techniques can be termed "clinical" because they would involve developing an in-depth profile of examinees' discourse skills on a case study basis.

A possible direction of development for new proficiency tests stems from already existing research on communicative competence by investigators such as Mehan who study the social organization of speech in particular kinds of activities. In Mehan's (1979) analysis of classroom recitation, the organization of a recurrent and important classroom encounter known as "lesson recitation" is mapped out as a network of interconnected roles played by teacher and a student. This network is shown below:

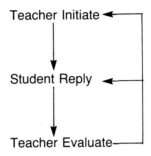

Teacher Initiate

Student Reply

Teacher Evaluate

Classroom recitation as a classroom activity is representative of a pattern of interactional relationships that most children who are successful in school must learn to recognize in terms of its demand on communication skills. Both teacher and student in enacting their roles in the lesson recitation script (to borrow a term from Duran, 1981, and Freedle & Duran, 1979) must understand how to modulate their language so as to meet the constraints and demands of the role each person plays.

In the Mehan (1979) account of the lesson recitation process each of the three major roles in the network of interaction may be fulfilled in communication by a relatively narrow range of speech acts which are contingent on each other in most circumstances. For example, if a teacher initiates conversation by asking a question, a child may reply with an answer, and this is likely to be followed by a teacher acknowledgement of the correctness of the child's reply, and so on.

Through extended observations of a child interacting with a teacher during lesson recitation it becomes potentially possible to summarize a child's communicative competence to participate in such an activity in terms of how well he or she fulfills different speech functions in interaction and how such fulfillments are marked linguistically. For example, it might be learned that a child's reply to a teacher's question is characteristically eliptical — one or two words only — and that, as a consequence, a teacher seldom has an opportunity to build up discussion of a topic without elaborate intervention. Qualitative information of this sort assembled into a profile for a child would prove valuable for diagnosing social-interactional skills in the child's repertoire and valuable in further understanding the consequences of the presence or absence of such skills in a child's overall communication effectiveness in a criterion setting.

Simplistic adoption of the technique described is dangerous. The work done by Carrasco, Vera & Cazden (1981) and Philips (1972) has amply illustrated that children's fluency in communication can be altered dramatically by changing the social characteristics of interlocutors without changing the basic referential demands of a communicative activity. Accordingly, development of a communicative profile of a speaker's effectiveness in a critical activity needs to be based on a deliberate manipulation or scheduled observation of communication where social participants vary and where other interactional parameters such as topic of discourse are allowed to vary. Full appreciation of how fluency in a communicative activity with known structure varies almost certainly will entail going beyond knowledge of the immediate contexts of an activity (such as a classroom) to knowledge about the social relations and culture which communicative participants are familiar with in other contexts. For the two reasons mentioned, development of a clinical proficiency profile technique based on communicative competence research can be seen as problematical. Nonetheless, it would appear that such a technique would be invaluable for use in assessing communication skills among persons whose circumstances dictate a careful assessment for their well-being. These circumstances might occur with children or adults who would otherwise be assessed as "alingual" or of very low proficiency in a language, or with children who show impairments in learning ability of unknown etiology. Another circumstance for reliance on a clinical profile methodology might be for use in assessing the professional qualifications of persons fulfilling critical social roles (e.g. census interviewer, social service interviewer, etc.), where ability to manage interaction successfully is an essential professional characteristic.

An important example of the use of communicative competence research techniques in functional evaluation of communication for practical purposes is exemplified by the evaluation system developed by Gumperz & Roberts (1978). This work using role play analysis evaluates adult non-native English speakers' skills in being interviewed for job placement. The techniques described appear particularly promising because they also are coupled with instruction of interviewees in how to manipulate discourse and prosodic cues to achieve communicative ends.

References

Bennett, A. T. 1980, Melodies bristling with change: Prosody and the understanding of conversation. *Sociological methods and research.*
Canale, M., & Swain, M. 1979, Communicative approaches to second language

teaching and testing. *Review and Evaluation Bulletin,* 1(5).

Carrasco, R., Vera, A., & Cazden, C. 1981, Aspects of bilingual students communicative competence in the classroom: A case study. In R. Duran (ed.), *Latino language and communicative behavior.* Norwood, N. J.: Ablex.

Clark, J. D. 1978, Psychometric considerations in language proficiency testing. In B. Spolsky (ed.), *Approaches to language testing.* Arlington, Va.: Center for Applied Linguistics.

Collins, J., & Michaels, S. 1980, The importance of conversational discourse strategies in the acquisition of literacy. *Berkeley Linguistic Society Series,* .

Cummins, J. 1980, The entry and exit fallacy in bilingual education. *NABE Journal,* 4(3), 25–60.

Duran, R. (ed.) 1981, *Latino language and communicative behavior.* Norwood, N. J.:Ablex.

Erikson, F. 1980, *Classroom discourse as improvisation.* Paper presented at the conference: Communicating in the Classroom, University of Wisconsin-Madison, October.

FSI (Foreign Service Institute) — ETS (Educational Testing Service). 1970, Foreign Service Institute Oral Interview Test. In *Manual for Peace Corps language testers.* Princeton, N. J.: ETS.

Freedle, R., & Duran, R. 1979, Sociolinguistic approaches to dialogue with suggested application to cognitive science. In R. Freedle (ed.), *New directions in discourse processing* (Vol. 2): *Advances in discourse processes.* Norwood, N. J.: Ablex.

Garcia, E. E. & Carrasco, R. 1981, An analysis of bilingual mother-child discourse. In R. Duran (ed.), *Latino language and communicative behavior.* Norwood, N. J.: Ablex.

Gleason, J. B. & Weintraub, S. 1978, Input language in the acquisition of communicative competence. In K. Nelson (ed.), *Children's language.* New York: John Wiley and Sons, Inc.

Grice, H. P. 1975, Logic and conversation. In P. Cole & J. L. Morgan (eds), *Syntax and semantics: Speech acts* (Vol. 3). New York: Academic Press.

Gumperz, J. J. & Kaltman, H. 1980, Prosody, linguistic diffusion and conversational inference. *Berkeley Linguistic Society Series.*

Gumperz, J. J. & Roberts, C. 1978, *Developing awareness skills for interethnic communication* (Report for limited circulation). Southall, Middlesex: National Centre for Industrial Language Training. (Available from National Centre for Industrial Language Training, Recreation Road, Middlesex, UB2, 5PF, England; Cost: £2.)

Gumperz, J. J. & Tannen, D. 1979, Individual and social differences in language use. In W. Wang & C. Fillmore (eds), *Individual differences in language ability and language behavior.* New York: Academic Press.

Lado, R. 1961, *Language testing: The construction and use of foreign language tests.* New York: McGraw Hill.

Mehan, H. 1979, *Learning lessons: Social organization in the classroom.* Cambridge, Mass.: Harvard University Press.

Oller, J. W. Jr. 1979, *Language tests at school: A pragmatic approach.* London: Longman Group, Ltd.

Oller, J. W. Jr., & Perkins, K. 1980, *Research in language testing.* Rowley, Mass.: Newbury House Publishers, Inc.

Philips, S. 1972, Participant structures and communicative competence: Warm Springs children in community and school. In C. B. Cazden, V. P. John & D. Hymes (eds), *Functions of language in the classroom*. New York: Teachers College Press.

Richards, J. C. 1980, Conversation. *TESOL Quarterly*, 14(4), 413–32.

Schegloff, E. & Sacks, H. 1973, Opening up closings. *Semiotica*, 8, 289–327.

Scollon, R. 1981, *The rhythmic integration of ordinary talk*. Paper presented at the meeting of the 32nd Annual Georgetown University Round Table on Language and linguistics, Washington, D.C., March.

Spolsky, B. (ed.) 1978, *Papers in applied linguistics: Advances in language testing series: 2*. Arlington, Va.: Center for Applied Linguistics.

Tarone, E. E. 1977, Conscious communication strategies: A progress report. In H. Douglas Brown, C. Yorio & R. Crymes (eds), *Teaching and learning English as a second language: Trends in research and practice: On TESOL '77: Selected papers from the Eleventh Annual Convention of TESOL*. Washington: TESOL.

PART II

Application

*In Ch Rivera (ed) (1984)
A Communicative Competence Approach
to Language Proficiency Assessment,
Multilingual Matters 9*

Linguistic interdependence among Japanese and Vietnamese immigrant students[1]

Jim Cummins
Ontario Institute for Studies in Education

Merrill Swain
Ontario Institute for Studies in Education

Kazuko Nakajima
University of Toronto

Jean Handscombe
North York Board of Education

Daina Green
Ontario Institute for Studies in Education

Chau Tran
North York Board of Education

Introduction

It is frequently argued in opposition to bilingual education in the United States that if language minority students are deficient in English then they need intensive instruction *in English*. Attempting to remedy English language deficiencies through instruction in students' first language (L1) appears counter-intuitive to many policymakers and educators. The implicit theoretical assumption underlying this position has been labelled the "Separate Underlying Proficiency" (SUP) model of bilingualism, in that proficiency in L1 and L2 (the second language) are assumed to be separate (Cummins, 1981a). This position is contrasted with the "Common Underlying Proficiency" (CUP) model of bilingualism in which L1 and L2 proficiency are assumed to be interdependent. The implication for bilingual education is that if L1 and L2 proficiency are manifestations of a common underlying proficiency, then instruction in either language is, theoretically, capable of promoting the proficiency underlying academic skills in both languages.

Cummins (1981a) has reviewed data from five areas which are consistent with the interdependence hypothesis. These areas are: (1) evaluations of bilingual education programs; (2) studies relating age to L2 acquisition; (3) investigations of the use of L1 in the home context when L2 is the language of schooling; (4) correlational studies of the relationship between L1 and L2; and (5) experimental studies of bilingual information processing.

The study reported here was designed to investigate the interdependence hypothesis among Japanese and Vietnamese immigrant students in Toronto, Canada. According to the interdependence hypothesis, older immigrant students whose L1 academic proficiency is better developed on arrival in Canada will acquire English academic skills more rapidly than younger immigrant students. The term "academic" or "context-reduced" language proficiency is being used to refer to aspects of language proficiency which are cognitively-demanding and are manifested in situations where the communicative activity is supported only by linguistic cues. At the other end of the continuum is "context-embedded" proficiency where a wide range of paralinguistic and situational cues support the communicative activity (See Cummins, 1981a, 1983; Swain, 1981, for a description of the theoretical model). The use of Japanese and Vietnamese immigrant students provides a stringent test of the interdependence hypothesis because of the considerable differences between English and these two languages. Also, the generalizability of the hypothesis is tested by the use of two groups of students with very different background characteristics, namely, upper-middleclass Japanese students and Vietnamese refugee students.

In addition to investigating the extent to which the acquisition of L2 academic proficiency is related to immigrant students' L1 proficiency on arrival, the following questions were also considered:

1. What is the relationship between level of L1 proficiency on arrival and continued development of L1?
2. How are academic aspects of L1 and L2 communicative proficiency related to other dimensions of communicative proficiency?

3. What is the influence of different background (e.g. personality characteristics, parental education) and behavioral (e.g. language use patterns) variables on the acquisition of English proficiency and maintenance of L1 proficiency?

The investigation of the interdependence hypothesis differed in important respects from the investigation of these latter three questions insofar as the researchers attempted to formally test predictions derived from the interdependence hypothesis whereas their approach to the other issues was essentially exploratory; in other words, for these issues the aim was to *generate*, rather than formally test hypotheses.

Method

Subjects

Japanese sample. An original sample of 91 high socioeconomic status Japanese students attending grades 2 and 3 and grades 5 and 6 of the School of Supplementary Japanese Studies (Saturday, 9 a.m.–2.35 p.m.) in Toronto was administered the group English and Japanese academic language proficiency measures. From this original sample 59 (32 male, 27 female) were administered the individual English academic measures and Japanese and English interviews. The subsample was selected in such a way that length of residence (LOR) and sex would be as similar as possible in older and younger groups. All parents were "temporary residents" who were in Canada for job-related reasons and who intended to eventually return to Japan. Thus, there was high motivation to maintain children's Japanese proficiency.

Vietnamese sample. School district records had suggested that there was an adequate number of Vietnamese L1 students enrolled in the district for the purpose of this study. However, after beginning to interview students it was discovered that although Vietnamese was their dominant language (as a result of schooling) and had been entered as "first language" in the school board computer, for many students Cantonese was their L1. Thus, the potential sample dwindled and eventually only 45 students were tested, 33 male and 12 female. It was possible to administer the English individual interview to 39 of these students.

All the Vietnamese students in the sample were recent arrivals, the LOR range being 5–22 months. The median age of the sample was 158 months with a range of 110–208 months. The researchers chose students between the ages of 9 and 17 years because they wanted to ensure that the sample had received some education in Vietnamese. Because of the fact that refugees often spent considerable periods of time in transit camps, a younger sample might have had little opportunity to develop Vietnamese literacy skills.

Data collection procedures

Japanese study. Although the School of Supplementary Japanese Studies was extremely cooperative in facilitating the selection of students, it was naturally unwilling to permit students to be tested during the limited class-time available to achieve their objectives. Since students lived in all areas of the city, testing during regular school hours was similarly unfeasible. Thus, the original sample was tested in late June and early July after regular Canadian school had started summer holidays. Testing was carried out in two locations (O.I.S.E. and a public school) and parents brought their child(ren) to the location most convenient to their homes. Five two-hour sessions were required to test all 91 students. Grade 2 and 3 students were tested in a different room from that of the grade 5 and 6 students. English and Japanese testing were separated by a short break for refreshments.

The subsample was selected during the summer and individual interviews with children and parents took place during September and October. Interviews were conducted in students' homes after regular school hours or on weekends. Two Japanese graduate assistants carried out the Japanese interviews while all English interviews were carried out by the same research officer (Daina Green). In some cases all three interviewers were involved in the home visits but usually both parent and child interviews were carried out by just one of the Japanese assistants.

All parent interviews were conducted in Japanese. Parents (almost invariably the mother) were provided with a form on which they filled in the more factual information with guidance from the graduate assistant. In some cases it turned out to be more efficient for the assistant to interview the parent and fill in the information herself. However in all cases the assistant was available to clarify and discuss the intention of the questions.

The English interviews with the children were conducted and recorded usually in a separate room while the parent was being interviewed. Then the children were interviewed in Japanese. Sometimes siblings were present and every effort was made to maintain an informal relaxed atmosphere. Some time was always spent in informal conversation with parent and child before any interviewing began. Interviews lasted usually about 15–20 minutes.

Vietnamese study. Because of the relatively small number of "genuine" Vietnamese L1 students in the North York school system, the researchers were forced to avail themselves of all students in the target age range, regardless of school or home location. Thus, it was not feasible to test during regular school hours because of the small number of students in any one school, and so groups of students (usually 5–10 at a time) were "ferried" to a central location (either O.I.S.E. or the North York Board of Education offices) for group testing and in some cases interviews. Group tests were given in both languages but individual interviews were conducted in English only by the same interviewer as in the Japanese study. (All children were recent arrivals and therefore fluent in Vietnamese.) In most cases the English interviews were conducted in students' homes several weeks after the group testing. During the group testing sessions children were provided with lunch and refreshments and most appeared to enjoy the experience. Between two and four adults were present at the testing sessions and the researchers tried to keep the ratio of children to adults at about 3 or 4:1.

Independent and dependent variables

Japanese study

Academic measures. The English academic measures consisted of the *Gates McGinitie grade 2 Vocabulary and Reading tests* (1979) a written *Prepositional Usage Test* (Wright & Ramsey, 1970) and orally administered adaptations of the Antonyms and Sentence Repetition subtests of the *Language Assessment Umpire* (LAU) (Cohen, 1980). These tests and the rationale for selecting them as measures of context-reduced or academic language proficiency are described in detail in Cummins, Swain, Nakajima, Handscombe, Green & Tran (1984).

Because the major aim of the School of Japanese Supplementary Studies is to develop the Japanese academic skills of expatriate children to a level commensurate with scholastic expectations in Japan, the researchers felt that it was appropriate to use a standardized test of reading skills normed on Japanese school children. The test that was chosen was the *Standardized Diagnostic Test of Reading Comprehension and Reading Proficiency Level I* (Grades 1, 2, 3) and *Level II* (Grades 4, 5, & 6) developed by Toshio Tatsumi (1968). The test is designed to provide a diagnostic assessment of reading skills from grade 1 through 6 and is widely used in Japan. There are four subtests: reading comprehension, usage, recognition of Chinese characters, and critical reading. Different levels of the test were given to grades 5 and 6 compared to grades 2 and 3. Scores were converted to T-scores with a mean of 50 and standard deviation of 10 based on Japanese norms. Because scores are expressed in relation to grade norms the age factor is effectively removed in the Japanese academic proficiency measure.

Interview measures. Because of the current fluid nature of the field of "communicative competence", it was decided not to make *a priori* judgements about its constituents. Instead an exploratory approach was adopted (influenced by the Canale & Swain, 1980 model) and an interview schedule was developed consisting of four phases (three in Japanese) each with somewhat different communicative demands.

The first phase of the English interview was a "warm-up" informal conversation which lasted for up to ten minutes; this was followed by a role-playing situation involving a toy telephone. This situation was included in an attempt to assess children's use of sociolinguistically appropriate forms. The third phase was a task in which children were required to place a series of 5 pictures in logical sequence and describe the story. This was included principally to provide opportunities for observing children's use of cohesive devices, a major aspect of discourse competence as described by Canale (this volume). The final phase was a picture description task which was intended to provide opportunities to observe children's strategic competence (Canale & Swain, 1980). The Japanese interview was similar except that the Picture Description phase was omitted because of time constraints.

Scoring procedures. In the absence of a detailed theory of the components of communicative proficiency in general and of the development of English proficiency among Japanese children in particular, the researchers decided to develop indices of communicative proficiency on the basis of the interview data themselves. Thus, the researchers listened to approximately 25% of the interviews, chosen at random, and developed and refined the scoring categories and scales based on specific aspects of the interviews which appeared to be particularly salient as well as more general aspects of children's communication (e.g. sophistication and accuracy of syntax, richness and detail of information communicated, extent to which child appeared at ease in the interview). Thus, ratings of inflectional use in English were included because problems in verbal inflections and plural markers characterized the speech of the Japanese children. The final scales in Japanese and English, therefore, represent a marriage between the Canale/Swain categories which guided the design of the interview and indices of proficiency which were dictated by the data themselves, or at least by the interpretations given to the data by the researchers.

The refinement of the English rating scales and the actual rating itself was carried out by the English interviewer (Daina Green) whose recollection of the interviews themselves with accompanying contextual and paralinguistic cues, undoubtedly influenced the scoring of several variables (such as interviewer speech). Because of this intense involvement with the data which obviously could not be matched by other raters, only one rating was obtained for the English interviews in the Japanese study.

For the Japanese interviews, however, two graduate assistants were involved and each scored five interviews conducted by the other. From the ten interviews scored by both assistants a total of 110 ratings each was available (10 students × 11 variables). There was exact agreement on 78% of these ratings and in no case did the discrepancy exceed one point. The indices of proficiency in English and Japanese are listed in the factor analyses presented in Tables 1 and 2 and are described in detail in Cummins *et al.* (1984).

Background variables. The parent interview yielded variables related to attributes and family background of the children as well as variables related to exposure, attitudes towards and use of both English and Japanese. The specific subcategories were Child Attributes (e.g. sex, personality [shy-outgoing] etc.), Parent Background, School Experiences in Canada, Parent-Related Language Behavior, Child Language Use and Preference, and Additional Exposure to Japanese and English. These variables were used in multiple regression analyses as predictors of English and Japanese proficiency.

Vietnamese study

Academic measures. The reading comprehension subtest of the grade 2 *Gates McGinitie Test* (1979) and the *English Prepositional Usage Test*[2], both used in the Japanese study, were also used in the Vietnamese study. In addition, 40-item oral English and Vietnamese Antonyms tests were developed such that 30 items in each test denoted concepts that were the same (or similar) in both languages. This procedure was intended to allow direct comparisons of students' performance across languages. The 40 items were derived through pilot testing from an original pool of about 95 words in each language.

Two Vietnamese written cloze tests were developed to further assess Vietnamese academic skills. One test (a fable) was considerably easier than the other (an expository passage). There were 22 blanks in the fable and 29 in the expository passage. Acceptable-word scoring procedures were used.

Interview. The English interview followed similar procedures to that of the Japanese study, although only the informal conversation and picture sequence phases were used and consequently scoring categories also differed somewhat. Data from the interview are reported in Cummins *et al.*, (1984) but will not be considered further here.

A detailed background interview was not carried out in the Vietnamese study although information was obtained from the children about last grade completed in Vietnam, whether they had studied English in camp, age and length of residence in Canada.

Data analysis

Japanese study. Analyses which were employed to test the interdependence hypothesis were partial correlational analysis, t-tests of the performance of older and younger students, and multiple regression analyses involving both the full Japanese sample of 91 students, and the subsample of 59 students for whom more complete data were available.

Within the subsample, exploratory factor analyses and multiple regression analyses were carried out to examine the relationships between context-embedded (interview) and context-reduced (academic) aspects of proficiency and also the relative influence on different aspects of proficiency of the *Background and Attributes* which children bring to the language learning situation on the one hand and their *Behavior and Exposure* to the language in that situation on the other.

In order to reduce the dependent variables to more manageable proportions for purpose of the regression analyses, Pearson product-moment correlations were computed and then factor analyses were carried out using the SPSS factor analysis program (Nie, Hull, Jenkins, Steinbrenner & Bent, 1975). For both English and Japanese analyses three factors with eigenvalues greater than one were obtained and were rotated to a varimax criterion. Factor scores (mean of zero and SD of 1) were then derived for each factor and were used as dependent variables in subsequent multiple regression analyses. Japanese academic proficiency was also included as a dependent variable in these regression analyses.

Vietnamese study. The interdependence hypothesis was tested in the Vietnamese study by computing Pearson and partial (controlling for length of residence) correlations between Vietnamese and English academic measures. Hierarchical multiple regression analyses were also carried out.

In presenting the results, the factor analyses of English and Japanese measures will be described first since the variables derived from these analyses were also used in most subsequent analyses.

Results

Japanese study.

Structure of proficiency. The first factor to emerge in the English analyses (Table 1) is defined by the three Syntax measures, the second by the three Richness measures and by Ease while the third factor is defined by the English Academic Proficiency measures. However, it can be seen that most of the academic proficiency measures show moderate loadings on Factors 1 and 2 in addition to Factor 3. The first two factors appear to correspond in a general way to the syntactic/morphological and pragmatic dimensions which Damico & Oller (1980) have distinguished in their research on children's language disorders. The fact that Picture Sequence Cohesion loads on Factor 2 rather than Factor 1 supports the distinction between grammatical and discourse or pragmatic competence (Canale, this volume, Bachman & Palmer, this volume). The pattern of loadings on these two factors suggests the labels Syntax (Factor 1) and Interactional Style (Factor 2). The third factor is labelled English Academic Proficiency.

TABLE 1 *Factor analysis of English academic language proficiency (17–21) and interview measures (1-16)*

Variables	Varimax rotation		
	1	*2*	*3*
1. Pronunciation	*0.69*	0.26	0.22
2. Interviewer speech	0.48	0.41	0.32
3. Semantically appropriate responses	0.17	*0.58*	0.22
4. Conversational richness	0.16	*0.77*	0.08
5. Inflections of verbs and nouns	*0.67*	0.14	*0.35*
6. Article use	*0.73*	0.24	0.20
7. Conversational syntax	*0.80*	0.23	0.44
8. Ease	0.23	*0.73*	0.16
9. Tel. question formation	*0.57*	0.31	0.26
10. Tel. appropriateness	0.39	0.20	0.48
11. Picture sequence syntax	*0.73*	0.22	0.44
12. Picture sequence cohesion	0.14	*0.62*	*0.52*
13. Picture sequence richness	0.32	*0.66*	0.31
14. Picture description syntax	*0.81*	0.36	0.33
15. Picture description strategies	*0.56*	0.49	0.25
16. Picture description richness	0.40	*0.64*	0.24
17. English vocabulary	0.46	0.33	*0.72*
18. English reading	0.39	0.29	*0.84*
19. English prepositions	0.34	0.17	*0.50*
20. English antonyms	*0.52*	0.41	*0.60*
21. Sentence repetition	0.49	*0.50*	*0.56*

In the Japanese analysis (Table 2), eight of the 12 variables have loadings of 0.50 or greater on Factor 1 and this factor appears to represent a general Japanese proficiency dimension. Factor 2 has high loadings from Japanese Academic Language Proficiency, Pronunciation and Fluency while the third factor is defined only by Use of English. These factor loadings become more intelligible when one realizes that Age is highly correlated with Factor 1 and length of residence (LOR) has a high negative correlation with Factor 2. This suggests that the variables loading on Factor 2 are those that are negatively affected by students' length of residence outside Japan, and this, rather than any intrinsic relationships, is what accounts for their presence on Factor 2. It should be remembered that Japanese Academic Language Proficiency is computed in relation to grade norms and this removal of age-related variance probably explains its low loading on the general Japanese factor.

The Japanese factor analysis suggests that communicative proficiency does not exist in a vacuum but rather its structure is sensitive to external influences. An implication is that attempts to empirically confirm models of communicative proficiency (e.g. Bachman & Palmer, this volume) cannot necessarily be generalized beyond the specific language learning context in which the data were gathered.

How is communicative proficiency related across languages?

Pearson and partial correlations between English and Japanese factor scores are presented in Table 3. Age and LOR were controlled in the

TABLE 2 *Factor analysis of Japanese academic language proficiency (1) and interview measures (2–12)*

Variables	Varimax rotation		
	1	*2*	*3*
1. Japanese academic language proficiency	0.23	*0.56*	0.01
2. Pronunciation	−0.09	*0.71*	0.23
3. Interviewer speech	*0.83*	0.10	0.04
4. Conversational richness	*0.78*	0.27	−0.29
5. Use of English	0.07	0.15	*0.68*
6. Fluency	0.38	*0.75*	0.02
7. No response	*0.75*	0.19	0.14
8. Conversational syntax	*0.71*	0.42	−0.10
9. Ease	*0.86*	0.12	−0.36
10. Tel. directions	*0.63*	0.06	0.08
11. Tel. appropriateness	*0.51*	0.25	0.13
12. Picture sequence richness	*0.67*	0.08	0.22

TABLE 3 *Correlations between English and Japanese factor scores*

Pearson correlations				Partial correlations		
				Controlling for: AGE LOR		
	EFAC1	EFAC2	EFAC3		EFAC1	EFAC2	EFAC3
JFAC1	−0.18	0.51	0.16	JFAC1	−0.24	0.50	−0.06
	(59)	(59)	(59)		(56)	(56)	(56)
	P = 0.09	P = 0.00	P = 0.12		P = 0.04	P = 0.00	P = 0.32
JFAC2	−0.31	−0.16	−0.18	JFAC2	0.04	0.06	−0.10
	(59)	(59)	(59)		(56)	(56)	(56)
	P = 0.01	P = 0.11	P = 0.09		P = 0.38	P = 0.33	P = 0.22
JFAC3	−0.04	−0.07	0.11	JFAC3	0.04	−0.05	0.14
	(59)	(59)	(59)		(56)	(56)	(56)
	P = 0.37	P = 0.30	P = 0.19		P = 0.40	P = 0.37	P = 0.16

partial correlations because of the influence of these variables on the Japanese (and English) factors. It can be seen that EFAC 2 (English Factor 2) is correlated highly with JFAC 1 (Japanese Factor 1) and that this correlation is quite robust, being uninfluenced by the partialling out of Age and LOR. EFAC 1 and JFAC 2 also show a significant Pearson correlation but this disappears when Age and LOR are controlled. A marginally significant negative correlation appears between EFAC 1 and JFAC 1 when Age and LOR are controlled, suggesting a slight tendency for children who devote time to maintaining Japanese to have less well-developed English conversational syntax.

The strong correlation between EFAC 2 and JFAC 1 can be understood in terms of the indices of proficiency which are common to both factors. Conversational Richness, Picture Sequence Richness and Ease load on both. Interviewer speech (i.e. modifications made by interviewer in terms of paraphrase and rate of speech) also has a high loading on JFAC 1 and a moderate (0.41) loading on EFAC 2.

Thus, the correlations seem to indicate that interactional style is interdependent across languages. In other words, a child who tends to volunteer information and provide detailed elaborate responses to questions in Japanese will tend to manifest the same types of linguistic behavior in English. One might expect this trait to be related to personality variables and the extent to which this is the case will be examined in a later section.

The lack of significant correlations between EFAC 3 and JFAC 2, both of which incorporate the academic language proficiency variables, is not surprising in view of the hybrid nature of JFAC 2, which has considerably higher loadings from Pronunciation and Fluency than from Japanese Academic Proficiency. In order to examine the interdependence hyupothesis, it is necessary to examine the relationships between Japanese Academic Proficiency and the English Academic Proficiency variables.

Is academic language proficiency interdependent across languages?

Three analytic procedures were used to test the interdependence hypothesis: first partial correlations, controlling for LOR, were computed between Japanese Academic Proficiency and Age on Arrival (AOA), on the one hand, and the English Academic Proficiency variables, both individually and as represented by EFAC 3, on the other. It is necessary to partial out LOR because it is positively related to the development of English Academic Proficiency, but negatively related to Japanese Academic Proficiency, thereby masking the relationships between Japanese and English Academic Proficiency.

The second procedure used to test the interdependence hypothesis was multiple regression analysis. The researchers examined the increment to explained variance in English Academic Proficiency attributable to entering variables indicative of Japanese Academic Proficiency in the regression equation after LOR. These analyses were carried out on the complete original sample (N = 91) with English Reading as the dependent variable and on the subsample (N = 59) with EFAC 3 as the dependent variable.

The third type of analysis involved examining the effects of group differences in age on arrival (AOA) on English proficiency variables. These analyses involved comparisons both between older and younger siblings and between grades 5/6 and 2/3 children. The researchers' hypothesis was that, with LOR controlled, older children would perform better on the cognitive academic measures. There were no significant differences in LOR between these comparison groups.

Partial correlations. It can be seen in Table 4 that, with one exception, all the correlations between English cognitive/academic measures and both Japanese Academic Language Proficiency and Age on Arrival are significant (using one-tailed tests) in the predicted direction. These correlations are clearly consistent with the interdependence hypothesis, especially since variance due to age has been removed from Japanese Academic Language Proficiency as a result of the necessity to express scores in relation to grade norms.

Regression analyses. In the regression analyses Age on Arrival (AOA) was dichotomized based on a median split and a dummy variable (AOA: older group) created to represent membership in the group of children who

TABLE 4 *Partial correlations between English academic language proficiency measures and both Japanese academic language proficiency and age on arrival controlling for length of residence*

Variable	Japanese academic language proficiency		Age on arrival	
	$N = 57$	$N = 88$	$N = 57$	$N = 88$
1. Vocabulary	0.42**	0.44**	0.22*[1]	0.30**
2. Reading	0.46**	0.52**	0.29*	0.38**
3. Prepositions	0.22*[1]	0.23*	0.25*[1]	0.30**
4. Antonyms	0.30**		0.37**	
5. Sentence repetition	0.31**		0.11	
6. EFAC3	0.33**		0.33**	

** $p<0.01$ (one-tailed)
* $p<0.05$ (one-tailed)
[1] $p>0.05$ two-tailed

arrived at older ages. Children who arrived in an English-speaking country at ages between 81 and 128 months were given a code of 1 while those who arrived between 12 and 80 months were given a code of zero.

It can be seen in Table 5 that in the larger sample, LOR accounted for 30% of the variance in English Reading. Japanese Academic Proficiency accounted for an additional 19% while AOA: older group and Age brought the total explained variance to 53%. In all, the cognitive/academic block accounted for an increment in explained variance of 23.85% after the effect of LOR was removed.

Less incremental variance is explained by the cognitive/academic predictors when this regression is carried out in the subsample ($N = 59$). LOR explains 39.4% of the variance in English Reading while the cognitive/academic block adds 14.9% to a total explained variance of 54.3%. It should be noted that when LOR is entered first into the regression equation any variance shared between LOR and L1 cognitive/academic variables is attributed to LOR. Thus, the estimate of the effects of L1 cognitive/academic variables is conservative.

TABLE 5 *Regression of English reading on LOR and cognitive/academic predictor variables ($N = 91$)*

	Multiple R	R square	Rsq change	Simple R
LOR	0.55	0.30	0.30	0.55
Japanese academic proficiency	0.70	0.49	0.19	0.23
AOA: older group	0.73	0.53	0.04	−0.03
Age	0.73	0.53	0.01	0.40

When EFAC 3 is used as the dependent variable for English Academic Proficiency (Table 6) the total explained variance drops to 35% with the cognitive/academic block explaining slightly more incremental variance (18%) than LOR (17%).

TABLE 6 *Regression of EFAC3 on LOR and cognitive/academic predictor variables (N = 59)*

	Multiple R	R square	Rsq change	Simple R
LOR	0.41	0.17	0.17	0.41
Japanese academic proficiency	0.51	0.26	0.09	0.18
AOA: older group	0.59	0.35	0.09	0.08
Age	0.59	0.35	0.00	0.41

In summary, it is clear from these regressions that students' level of L1 cognitive/academic development makes a considerable difference in the rapidity with which L2 cognitive/academic proficiency is developed. Despite the fact that the languages are so different, Japanese Academic Proficiency by itself adds 19% to the explanation of variance in English Reading (Table 5). The researchers regard these results as rather strong evidence for the interdependence hypothesis and the existence of a common underlying proficiency. Clearly, however, there is considerable variance left unexplained and the extent to which this variance can be accounted for by other variables will be examined in a later section.

Sibling and age group comparisons. There were 14 sets of siblings in the subsample (N = 59). Differences between older and younger siblings were analysed by means of correlated t tests. Significant differences (p<0.01) were found in favor of older siblings on English Vocabulary, English Reading and Antonyms, and differences approached significance (p<0.10) on Prepositions and Sentence Repetition. Differences were also apparent on most of the Japanese variables which loaded on JFAC1. On a large majority of the context-embedded English variables differences did not attain significance.

The results of the sibling analyses were supported by comparisons of grade 5/6 (N = 30) and 2/3 (N = 24) students using t tests for independent samples. Significant (p 0.05) differences in favor of older students were observed on four out of five (80%) English context-reduced tasks but on the context-embedded tasks differences reached significance in only four out of 16 (25%) cases. These findings support the interdependence hypothesis but are inconsistent with suggestions that older children make more rapid progress in all aspects of L2 acquisition (e.g. Krashen, Long & Scarcella, 1979).

On the Japanese variables older students performed better on all but Pronunciation and Use of English. These findings are corroborated by the results of the parent interviews where 68% of the grades 2 and 3 children's parents reported errors in their children's present Japanese speech, whereas only 43% of the grades 5 and 6 children's parents reported similar errors despite the fact that mean LOR was somewhat longer for the older students. These findings suggest that level of Japanese proficiency on arrival in Canada may be an important factor in maintaining the language.

In summary, the results of all the analyses carried out are consistent with the interdependence hypothesis, namely, that development of L2 cognitive/academic (context-reduced) proficiency is partially a function of level of L1 cognitive/academic proficiency at the time intensive exposure to L2 begins. The findings also suggest that older immigrant students maintain and develop their L1 skills better than students who immigrate at a younger age. It is significant that despite the vast difference in subjects (Japanese upper-class versus Finnish working-class) and contexts, this pattern of results is precisely the same as that reported by Skutnabb-Kangas & Toukomaa (1976), namely level of L1 proficiency on arrival is important both for acquisition of L2 academic proficiency and for continued development of L1 academic proficiency.

However, L1 cognitive/academic proficiency is only one factor influencing the acquisition of L2 proficiency. It remains to be seen what other factors are important and to what extent distinct sets of predictor variables *differentially* affect the acquisition of different aspects of L2 proficiency as well as the continued development of Japanese proficiency.

Prediction of English and Japanese proficiency. A set of 28 variables derived largely from the parent interviews was grouped into two major blocks, the first related to the Background (e.g. Mother's Education) and Attributes (e.g. Personality) of the children and the second related to Exposure to and Behavior relevant to the acquisition of English or Japanese (e.g. LOR, Child Language to Siblings). Two additional variables within the Attributes block, namely, JFAC1 and Japanese Academic Proficiency, were included in English regression analyses.

The order of entry of the two blocks into the equation was varied in order to estimate how much variance could be accounted for uniquely by each block in the different dependent variables. These analyses are presented in Table 7. What is of primary interest here is not the total amount of variance explained, which may not be stable due to the relatively small number of subjects, but the relative importance of what children bring to the language learning situation as compared to their actual experiences in that situation.

TABLE 7 *Cumulative amount of variance (R^2) in English and Japanese proficiency explained by background/attributes and exposure/behavior blocks*

	EFAC1	EFAC2	EFAC3	JFAC1	JFAC2	JFAC3	Japanese academic proficiency
Background/attributes	33	45	39	46	35	29	30
Exposure/behavior (E/B)	95	75	77	65	84	57	73
E/B unique: (a) increment	62	30	38	19	49	28	43
(b) % of total	65	40	49	29	58	49	59
Exposure/behavior	76	48	48	32	71	39	52
Background/attributes (B/A)	95	75	77	65	84	57	73
B/A unique: (a) increment	19	27	29	33	13	18	21
(b) % of total	20	36	38	51	15	32	29

It is clear that the Exposure/Behavior block exerts a greater impact on EFAC1 than on either EFAC2 or EFAC3 (65% of explained variance accounted for uniquely versus 40% and 49%), whereas the Background Attributes block accounts for more of the explained variance in EFAC2 and EFAC3 than on EFAC1 (36% and 38% unique variance respectively versus 20%).

For the Japanese measures the greater proportions of variance accounted for by the Background/Attributes block in JFAC1 and by the Exposure/Behavior block in JFAC2 can be attributed largely to the effects of Personality (shy-outgoing scale), Age and Age on Arrival on JFAC1 and LOR on JFAC2.

The relative influence of Exposure and Attributes on the acquisition of English was examined in a reduced model involving seven variables (Table 8). Exposure is represented by LOR, Cognitive/Academic Attributes by variables 2–4 and Other Personal Attributes by variables 5-7. After LOR is entered into the equation, Attributes account for an increment in explained variance of 10%, 27% and 21% in EFAC1, EFAC2 and EFAC3 respectively. However, for EFAC2, Cognitive/Academic variables account for only 5% increment while other Personal attributes account for 21%. For EFAC3 the pattern is reversed, with 18% and 3% incremental variance accounted for by these two blocks.

The findings of the regression analyses suggest that individual differences do not greatly affect acquisition of L2 syntax as manifested in informal conversation. Exposure to and use made of the language appear to be considerably more important. However, L2 Interactional Style and L2 Cognitive/Academic Proficiency appear to be affected to a much greater extent by the personal attributes individuals bring with them to the task of acquiring L2. Specifically, personality and L1 interactional style play a major role in determining the ways in which learners tend to interact in L2 whereas L1 cognitive/academic maturity exerts an important influence on the rapidity with which L2 cognitive/academic skills are developed. This latter issue was further investigated in the Vietnamese study.

Vietnamese study

Pearson correlations among English and Vietnamese academic proficiency variables (Table 9) show highly significant relationships both within and across languages. With the exception of some correlations involving the Prepositions task the intra- and inter-language correlations are all significant at less than the 0.01 level. Partialling out LOR increased the English-Vietnamese correlations somewhat. The strong positive correlations between Age and Last grade in Vietnam on the one hand and

TABLE 8 *Exposure and attribute predictors of English proficiency*

	EFAC1			EFAC2			EFAC3		
	R square	Rsq change	Beta	R square	Rsq change	Beta	R square	Rsq change	Beta
	0.26	0.26	0.54	0.21	0.21	0.49	0.17	0.17	0.73
1. LOR	0.26	0.00	0.13	0.25	0.04	0.11	0.26	0.09	0.25
2. Japanese academic proficiency	0.28	0.02	-0.06	0.27	0.01	0.06	0.35	0.09	0.40
3. AOA: older group	0.29	0.01	-0.05	0.27	0.00	-0.14	0.35	0.00	0.08
4. Age in months	0.30	0.01	-0.03	0.32	0.05	0.09	0.37	0.01	-0.09
5. Personality*	0.33	0.03	-0.21	0.44	0.12	0.42	0.37	0.01	-0.11
6. JFAC1	0.36	0.02	-0.16	0.48	0.04	0.21	0.38	0.01	0.07
7. Sex**									

* 5 point scale, 1 = very shy, 5 = very outgoing
** 2 = Female, 1 = Male

TABLE 9 *Correlation matrix for English and Vietnamese academic proficiency measures*

	1	2	3	4	5	6	7	8	9	10
1. Age	1.00									
2. LOR	-0.11	1.00								
3. V antonyms	0.64	-0.17	1.00							
4. V cloze 1	0.39	-0.18	0.60	1.00						
5. V cloze 2	0.64	-0.30	0.90	0.68	1.00					
6. E reading	0.66	0.11	0.68	0.41	0.51	1.00				
7. E prepositions	0.39	0.24	0.45	-0.06	0.23	0.54	1.00			
8. E. antonyms	0.61	0.25	0.69	0.43	0.52	0.83	0.51	1.00		
9. Last grade in Vietnam	0.88	-0.35	0.84	0.65	0.78	0.63	0.23	0.60	1.00	
10. Sex	-0.23	-0.27	-0.52	-0.39	-0.45	-0.22	0.02	-0.16	-0.50	1.00

English and Vietnamese proficiency variables on the other, provide further support for the interdependence hypothesis.

The hierarchical regression analysis presented in Table 10 shows that L1 cognitive/academic proficiency strongly predicts L2 cognitive/academic proficiency. Cognitive maturity, insofar as it is represented by Age is also strongly related to L1 cognitive/academic proficiency. The fact that LOR accounts for considerably less variance than in the Japanese study is probably due to its smaller range in the Vietnamese sample. However, it is worth noting that in the Vietnamese study LOR generally accounted for more variance on the English interview dependent variables than on the academic dependent variables, whereas the L1 cognitive/academic block showed the opposite pattern. This trend was also evident in the Japanese study.

TABLE 10 *Predictors of English and Vietnamese academic proficiency*

Variables	E antonyms			V antonyms		
	R square	Rsq change	Beta	R square	Rsq change	Beta
1. LOR	0.06	0.06	0.35	0.03	0.03	−0.03
2. V antonyms	0.61	0.56	0.67			
3. Age	0.66	0.05	0.26	0.42	0.39	0.55
4. Sex	0.68	0.02	0.17	0.55	0.13	−0.38

In summary, the findings of the Vietnamese study provide further strong evidence for the interdependence hypothesis.

Discussion and conclusions

The interdependence hypothesis. In both studies it was found that L1 cognitive/academic proficiency accounted for a highly significant proportion of variance in L2 cognitive/academic proficiency, as predicted by the interdependence hypothesis. The Japanese study also provided evidence that immigrant children who arrived in Canada at older ages maintained and/or continued to develop L1 cognitive/academic skills to a greater extent than younger immigrant children.

The fact that the same pattern of findings emerged among two such dissimilar samples suggests the robustness of the interdependence hypothesis. The hypothesis is also supported by recent findings (Robson, 1981) that both previous formal education and literacy in Hmong (L1) independently predicted progress in learning English in a formal classroom setting among Hmong refugees in Southeast Asian camps.

Parallel findings to those of the present study have been reported by Skutnabb-Kangas & Toukomaa (1976). They found age on arrival in Sweden was important both for the acquisition of Swedish academic proficiency and for continued development of Finnish academic proficiency. Also, Snow & Hoefnagel-Höhle (1978) reported a significant advantage for older English L1 immigrant children (and adults) acquiring Dutch as a second language and noted a tendency for younger children to replace English with Dutch:

"With one exception (a 7 year-old-girl), it was only among the 3–5 year old Beginners (and among the 6–7 year-old Advanced subjects, who had learned Dutch while 3–5 years old) that growing control of Dutch was associated with breakdown of control of English. Although a few subjects in all age groups showed some degree of negative interference, mostly at the lexical level, from Dutch into English, large decreases in English fluency and a preference for speaking Dutch were observed only among the youngest subjects". (1978, p. 1126)

Thus the present findings agree with those of other studies in showing that older immigrant students whose L1 proficiency is better established at the time of intensive exposure to L2, not only make more rapid progress in acquiring academic aspects of L2, but also maintain and develop their L1 more adequately than students who immigrate at younger ages. This does not mean that older immigrant students will necessarily attain higher ultimate levels of L2 than younger students, since LOR is also an extremely important factor. The findings of Cummins (1981b) suggests that the effects of LOR tend to diminish after 5 years and thus, in terms of immigrant students' ability to approach grade norms in L2 academic skills, there may be a critical age on arrival at about age 12, after which it will become increasingly difficult for students to catch up.

The nature of L2 proficiency. Although this study is essentially exploratory, the pattern of findings from the factor analysis and regression equations suggest a distinction between Attribute-based and Input-based aspects of L2 proficiency. Attribute-based proficiency refers to those aspects of L2 proficiency which are strongly related to personal characteristics of the individual (e.g. personality or cognitive traits). Input-based proficiency, on the other hand, refers to those aspects of proficiency in which individual differences are determined primarily by differential exposure to "comprehensible input" (Krashen, 1981) with stable attributes of the individual accounting for relatively little variance.

This conceptualization allows the interdependence hypothesis to be placed into a broader framework insofar as all attribute-based aspects of proficiency will be interdependent across languages. This would not be the case for input-based aspects of proficiency. The model of attribute-based proficiency suggested by the present findings is shown in Figure 1.

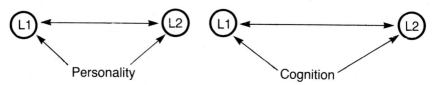

FIGURE 1   *Model of Attribute-Based Interdependent Language Proficiency*

Essentially the model proposes that L1 and L2 interactional style (EFAC2) are interdependent as a result of the fact that both are, to a significant extent, manifestations of personality attributes of the individual. Similarly, L1 and L2 cognitive/academic proficiency are interdependent as a result of the fact that both are, to a significant extent, manifestations of the same underlying cognitive proficiency.

The major implications for assessment of language proficiency are that the construct of proficiency is not unitary and that traditional distinctions and modes of assessment (e.g. listening, speaking, reading, and writing) may be less fundamental than distinctions related to the context in which the communicative activity takes place (i.e. context-embedded vs. context-reduced) and the extent to which communicative performance is determined by relatively stable attributes of the individual.

Notes

1.   The research reported in this paper was funded by InterAmerica Research Associates, Inc. The paper is based on a report of the same title published by the National Clearinghouse for Bilingual Education in 1982. We would like to express our appreciation to all the students, parents and teachers who cooperated so willingly in the project and to the many colleagues who provided advice and concrete assistance at various stages. We also want to thank Chieko Inoue and Takako Shimizu who collected the Japanese language data, Lan Nguyen who helped collect the Vietnamese data and John Arce and Mary Lou King who carried out the data analyses. Finally we owe a special debt of gratitude to Charlene Rivera, our project officer at InterAmerica for her patience and support throughout the project.

2.   The *English Prepositional Usage Test* was developed in 1969 by E. N. Wright and C. A. Ramsey for the Toronto Board of Education.

References

Canale, M., & Swain, M. 1980, Theoretical bases of communicative approaches to second language teaching and testing. *Applied Linguistics*, 1(1), 1–47.

Cohen, B. 1980, *Language assessment umpire*. New York: Santillana.

Cummins, J. 1981a, The role of primary language development in promoting educational success for language minority students. In California State Department of Education (ed.), *Schooling and language minority students: A theoretical framework*. Los Angeles: National Dissemination and Assessment Center.

—— 1981b, Age on arrival and immigrant second language learning in Canada: A reassessment. *Applied Linguistics*, 2(2), 132–49.

—— 1984, Wanted: A theoretical framework for relating language proficiency to academic achievement among bilingual students. In C. Rivera (ed.) *Language proficiency and academic achievement*. Clevedon, England: Multilingual Matters.

Cummins, J., Swain, M., Nakajima, K., Handscombe, J., Green, D. & Tran, C. 1984, *Linguistic interdependence among Japanese and Vietnamese immigrant students*. Toronto: National Heritage Language Resource centre.

Damico, J. S. & Oller, J. W., Jr. 1980, Pragmatic versus morphological/syntactic criteria for language referrals. *Language Speech and Hearing Services in Schools*, 11, 85–94.

Krashen, S. 1981, *Second language acquisition and second language learning*. London: Pergamon Press.

Krashen, S. D., Long, M. A. & Scarcella, R. C. 1979, Age, rate and eventual attainment in second language acquisition. *TESOL Quarterly*, 13, 573–82.

McGinitie, W. H. 1979, *Gates-McGinitie Reading Test, Level B., Form 2* (Canadian ed.). Toronto: Thomas Nelson.

Nie, N. H., Hull, C. H., Jenkins, J. G., Steinbrenner, K. & Bent, D. H. 1975, *Statistical package for the social sciences* (2nd ed.). New York: McGraw-Hill.

Robson, B. 1981, *Alternatives in ESL and literacy: Ban Vanai* (Final report to Asia Foundation). Washington, D.C.: Center for Applied Linguistics, May. (Asia Foundation Grant #SF-110-SF0039)

Skutnabb-Kangas, T., & Toukomaa, P. 1976, *Teaching migrant children's mother tongue and learning the language of the host country in the context of the socio-cultural situation of the migrant family*. Helsinki: The Finnish National Commission for UNESCO.

Snow, C. E. & Hoefnagel-Höhle, M. 1978, The critical period for language acquisition: Evidence from second language learning. *Child Development*, 49, 1114–1128.

Swain, M. 1981, Bilingual education for majority and minority language children. *Studio Linguistica*, 35, 15–32.

Tatsumi, T. 1968, *Standardized diagnostic test of reading comprehension and reading proficiency. Levels I and II*. Tokyo: Kaneko Shobo.

Wright, E. N. & Ramsey, C. A. 1970, *Students of non-Canadian origin: Age on arrival, academic achievement and ability* (Research report #88). Toronto: Toronto Board of Education.

Pupil characteristics and performance on linguistic and communicative language measures[1]

Arnulfo G. Ramírez
State University of New York at Albany

The study of language proficiency of bilingual students (e.g. Dulay & Burt, 1980) and its relationship to the goals of bilingual education and aspects of cognitive functioning (e.g. Duncan & De Avila, 1979) has received considerable attention in research in the area of bilingualism and bilingual education. While the contrasting concepts of linguistic vs. communicative competence have been influential in language teaching and language testing for quite some time, strict applications of this distinction in the measurement of bilingualism is a relatively recent phenomenon (e.g. John-Steiner, 1979; Legaretta, 1979; Rosansky, 1980).

The study

The purpose of this study is to attempt to: (1) clarify the relationship between communicative and linguistic competence within English (L2) and Spanish (L1) and across the two languages; (2) determine the relationship of linguistic and communicative competence to pupil achievement; and, (3) examine the extent to which pupil characteristics (home language use, self-concept, cognitive style, years in the U.S. and sex) influence performance on linguistic and communicative competence tests.

Measurement of linguistic and communicative competence

The definition of linguistic competence is relatively unproblematic as demonstrated by Legaretta's statement that "linguistic competence is the mastery of the sound system, semantics and basic structural patterns of a language" (1979, p. 523). However, definitions of communicative competence such as the "ability to adapt the totality of one's communicative resources, both linguistic and functional [(i.e. extra-linguistic and paralinguistic) to a given situation" (Legaretta, 1979, p. 523)] are often relatively broad. Recent attempts undertaken by communication experts (Wiemann

& Backlund, 1980) or applied linguists (Canale & Swain, 1980) to define the concept of communicative competence have only demonstrated the multiplicity of its possible components. At least three distinct traditions of inquiry are merging: (1) in the psychologists' and communication specialists' view, communicative competence, primarily, is seen as the ability to understand, organize and convey information (e.g. Flavell *et al.*, 1968; Wang, Rose & Marwell, 1973); (2) in the tradition of philosophers of language like Austin (1962) or Searle (1969), communicative competence is viewed as the ability to perform, speech acts efficiently; (3) in the sociolinguistic tradition, itself often influenced by the philosophy of language, defines communicative competence with regard to situational appropriateness of language use (Hymes 1971; Shuy 1979).

The testing of communicative competence is a very active and prolific field. While less than a decade ago communicative competence testing was still a relatively new field (Savignon, 1972; Briere, 1971), it is now a much discussed area of research (e.g. see Briere, 1979; Davies, 1978; Morrow, 1977). The measurement of communicative competence faces many problems, some of them related to the vagueness of the concept or trait to be measured. The measurement problems are compounded by the fact that the usual measurement of communicative competence is based on global rating scale approaches, while linguistic competence is generally measured in tests using a discrete item method. As a result, the suggestion has been made that in many situations a presumed difference between measured linguistic and communicative competence may reflect a difference in method of measurement rather than in the trait or constructs being measured (e.g. Corrigan & Upshur, 1978; Stevenson, 1979).

In order to avoid a method trait confusion, the data concerning both linguistics and communicative competence are based on discrete-point measurement. The linguistic competence measure utilized in this study was the *Bahia Oral Language Test* (*BOLT,* Cohen, Cruz & Bravo, 1976). The test consists of 20 items designed to elicit specific structures with a wide range of complexity. The structures are elicited by a combination of pictorial and verbal cues. English and Spanish versions of the tests are designed to be equivalent. Three measures of communicative proficiency Active Communicative Competence (ACC), Receptive Communicative Competence (RCC) and Sociolinguistic Competence (SC) were undertaken.

Active Communicative Competence was measured in a test involving four tasks: (1) Transmitting Information — students were asked to describe simple line drawings (e.g. apples falling from a tree) in such a way that the picture could be reproduced by an interlocutor who could not see the picture; (2) Giving Directions — involved giving directions that would enable another person to find his or her way to a party; (3) Giving Instructions — consisted of extending an invitation to a party on the basis of pictorial information (time indication, address, picture of projected activities) made available to the testee; and (4) Giving Descriptions — the reporting of an accident depicted in a series of line drawings. Scoring of the test was based on a content analysis of each task. That is, the description of the picture or the events of the accident was analyzed into smaller units of information with each unit forming a descrete item of the test. The replies of the testees were taped and then scored by examiners who checked each bit of information on the task analysis sheet as the information appeared in the examiner's reply. This procedure of analyzing student replies turned out to be nearly "objective." Variation in test scores obtained by three different examiners were minor and agreement (checked for 5 different students) was in the 90 to 99% range. An example of the ACC testing procedure is given in Appendix A.

Receptive Communicative Competence was defined as the ability to follow directions or instructions. Its measurement consisted of three components: (1) following directions on a map; (2) filling out a standardized form; and (3) following instructions by underlining and circling words in a written text. Each task was treated as a discrete item and the scoring of this test was entirely objective (see Appendix B for an example of the testing procedure for RCC).

Sociolinguistic Competence (SC) was defined as the ability to recognize the intent of speech acts. It was tested by a receptive, discrete item test. The stem of each item described the communicative intent of a teacher or pupil in a specific classroom situation. The stem was followed by four choices, two of which constituted possible ways of expressing the intended speech act. In one of the two correct choices the speech act was expressed overtly; in the other it was stated in a covert manner (see Appendix C for a sample item). Overt and covert speech act recognitions were scored as separate test items. Thus, the test led to a double score: overt and covert speech act recognition. The overt speech acts were expected to be recognized more easily than covert ones. The difference between the SC covert and SC overt scores was expected to furnish an indication of sociolinguistic sensitivity.

Variables related to language proficiency

In addition to assessing language proficiency, an attempt was made to measure such variables as (1) home language use, (2) cognitive style, (3) self-concept, and (4) school achievement.

The cognitive style measure employed was the *Group Embedded Figure Test (GEFT)* (Ottman, Raskins & Witkin, 1971). It is a perceptual test which requires subjects to identify a previously seen figure within a larger complex figure (Witkin, Ottman, Raskin & Karp, 1971) and is designed to measure field independence. The large and complex literature concerning field independence has been recently summarized by Duncan & De Avila (1979, pp. 22 ff.). Field dependence or field sensitivity is assumed by some (e.g. Ramírez & Castañeda, 1974) to be a cognitive style associated with socialization into traditional Mexican-American culture, while typical American mainstream schooling and socialization patterns tend to favor field independence. In a recent study, Duncan & De Avila (1979, pp. 27 ff.) have considered field independence not only as a cognitive style but as an ability associated with higher levels of language proficiency.

Self-concept was tested because of the importance attached to it within the overall rationale for bilingual education which links affirmation and/or preservation of home language and culture with enhancement of self-concept and increased academic achievement. The self-concept measure used was an instrument produced by Arias (1976). The instrument measures self-concept by recording agreement or disagreement with statements such as: "It's fun to be me" or "I feel unsure of myself in school." It is essentially an adaptation of a widely used instrument by Coopersmith (1967), but attempts to correct the cultural bias inherent in the Coopersmith and related self-concept measurement (e.g. Zirkel, 1971) by adjusting the instrument to a Mexican-American value system.

The only objective measure of school achievement available for high school students was the number of graduation-related competencies passed by the bilingual pupils. These competencies are measured by specific tests or subtests which, according to recent New York State legislation, must be passed by any student as a prerequisite for graduation from high school. Scores on the *CTBS (California Test of Basic Skills —* Reading, Language Arts, Math, McGraw-Hill, 1974) and the *CAT (California Achievements Test —* Vocabulary, Reading, Math, etc., Tiegs & Clark, 1970) were used as achievement measures for elementary school pupils.

Home language use was established by asking students to indicate the extent to which they utilized Spanish or English in the home domain. Exclusive use of Spanish corresponded to a 4, mostly Spanish and some English equalled a 3, mostly English and some Spanish were designated 2, and English only was equated to 1 on the scale.

Figure 1 illustrates the three major components of the study and the possible interrelationships among the specific variables;

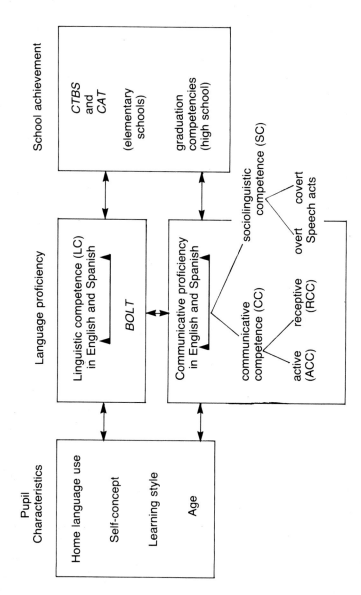

FIGURE 1 *Pupil characteristics and performance*

Description of the sample

The subjects used in the study included pupils from four different schools:

San Francisco Bay area schools
School 1 (Senior High School. N = 65)
Students were in a Spanish/English bilingual program; Approximately one third had been born in the U.S., another third had lived in the U.S. between 4–8 years, and a third were recent arrivals (1–2 years) from Latin America (primarily Mexico).
School 2 (Bilingual Elementary School, N = 18)
Students were in the 4th and 5th grades.
School 3 (Monolingual Elementary School, N = 32)
Students were mainly in the 4th and 5th grades and were English dominant.
Los Angeles area
School 4 (Bilingual Elementary School, N = 28)
Students were in the 4th and 5th grades.
(The Active Communicative Competence measures were not administered to these pupils.)

The three schools from the San Francisco Bay area were selected because they belonged to the same school district and were participants in a Teacher Corps Project with which the researcher was associated as a university faculty member. The Los Angeles bilingual school (School 4) was chosen to contrast with School 2.

Test administration and scoring

All students were tested in both English and Spanish between January and May 1980. The linguistic competence measure, *BOLT* (Cohen, Cruz & Bravo, 1976) was administered first followed by three tests of communicative proficiency. The *BOLT* and the test for active communicative competence were administered individually by bilingual graduate assistants. The measures assessing receptive communicative competence and sociolinguistic competence were administered to groups of students at the four schools.

The *BOLT* was scored according to the directions in the test manual — one point for each correct item. The test measuring active communicative competence scoring was scored on the basis of the amount and accuracy of information provided by each student. One point was assigned for each detail in a given task. The amount/accuracy of information notion was selected because it is believed that this criteria is often used by teachers in evaluating their pupils. In addition, this approach was efficient in terms of scoring time and high inter-rater reliability. For the RCC, one point was assigned for each instruction or directive successfully completed by the student. Similarly, for the SC, one point was given for the correct overt and covert act in each item. A difference score (total correct overt vs. total correct covert) was also computed.

Reliability of the linguistic and communicative measures

To establish the internal consistency of the language proficiency tests, Cronback's alpha coefficient was calculated on the basis of all complete data sets for subjects in the San Francisco Bay Area and Los Angeles schools. The results are presented in Table 1.

TABLE 1 *Means, standard deviations and reliability of language tests for San Francisco and Los Angeles school sites*

Test	Number of students	Maximum score	Mean	Standard deviation	Cronback's Alpha
San Francisco					
1. BOLT-English	111	20	15.50	4.55	0.90
2. BOLT-Spanish	92	20	11.79	8.34	0.98
3. ACC-English	50	77	39.04	12.55	0.94 (75 items)
4. RCC-English	48	25	16.08	5.53	0.89
5. SC-overt English	91	20	18.23	4.08	0.95
6. SC-covert English	90	20	17.51	4.00	0.95
7. ACC-Spanish	38	78	40.50	12.04	0.93 (71 items)
8. RCC-Spanish	39	20	11.56	5.22	0.90
9. SC-overt Spanish	87	20	12.55	8.06	0.98
10. SC-covert Spanish	87	20	11.83	7.62	0.97
Los Angeles					
1. BOLT-English	28	20	14.79	3.97	0.97
2. BOLT-Spanish	28	20	16.04	3.32	1.00
3. RCC-English	28	25	13.36	3.62	0.81
4. SC-overt English	28	20	19.25	1.78	0.85
5. SC-covert English	28	20	17.02	3.02	0.85
6. RCC-Spanish	28	20	11.36	1.87	0.80
7. SC-overt Spanish	28	20	18.89	2.03	0.79
8. SC-covert Spanish	28	20	17.75	2.42	0.73

The reliability for the *BOLT* measure was 0.90 (San Francisco) and 0.97 (Los Angeles) for the English version and 0.98 (San Francisco) and 1.00 (Los Angeles) for the Spanish version. The reliability for the communicative competence tests ranged from 0.81 (Los Angeles) to 0.89 (San Francisco) for the RCC-English; 0.80 (Los Angeles) to 0.90 (San Francisco) for the RCC-Spanish; 0.94 for the ACC-English and 0.93 for the ACC-Spanish. The reliabilities for the measure assessing sociolinguistic competence was extremely high for the San Francisco sites (English 0.95 overt and 0.95 covert Spanish: 0.98 overt and 0.97 covert). The results were partly due to a lack of variance and/or the ceiling effects of the test. For example, means were 18.23 (out of 20) for the overt English and 17.51 (out of 20) for the covert English. In the reliabilities for the Los Angeles administration, the same ceiling effect was apparent in both languages, but the reliabilities were lower (Spanish: 0.79 overt and 0.73 covert; English: 0.85 overt and 0.85 covert). It appears that item format (selecting two out of four choices) on the SC measure greatly influenced pupil performance and, in turn, contributed to a lack of difficulty for many students at both the elementary and high school levels.

Because both the English and Spanish measures of active communicative competence measure the amount/accuracy of information and could be subject to evaluator subjectivity, inter-rater reliability was calculated using specific scoring guidelines developed by the project staff. Three trained raters scored the same ten tapes (ACC-English) independently and agreement was found to be between 0.90 and 0.95.

Findings

Correlations between linguistic and communicative measures

The relationship between the linguistic and communicative measures varied greatly among the four schools. A summary of the results is presented for each school:

School 1 (High School)

Table 2 shows the intercorrelation of all the linguistic proficiency measures. All of the English proficiency measures devised for this study correlated highly (p.<001) with linguistic competence in English. Covert and overt SCT in both languages correlate so highly (0.92) that they can be assumed to measure the same ability.

The high correlation between linguistic competence and ACC in English should not be interpreted to mean that the tests measure the same variable. A preliminary examination of scatter plots reveals that (1) a certain amount of linguistic competence is, of course, the prerequisite for communicative competence but that (2) even at relatively low or relatively high levels of linguistic competence there can be considerable variance in

TABLE 2 Correlations of linguistic and communicative competence measures for school 1

Correlations measure	1	2	3	4	5	6	7	8	9	10
1. BOLT English	*									
2. BOLT Spanish	−0.15	*								
3. SC-covert English	−0.69***	−0.22	*							
4. SC-overt English	−0.61***	−0.26	0.92***	*						
5. ACC-English	0.67***	−0.34*	0.41**	0.38**	*					
6. RCC-English	0.78***	−0.08	0.77***	0.68***	0.58***	*				
7. SC-covert Spanish	−0.12	0.20	−0.11	−0.14	−0.08	−0.10	*			
8. SC-overt Spanish	−0.17	0.34*	−0.16	−9.07	−0.14	−0.12	0.92***	*		
9. ACC-Spanish	0.45**	0.17	0.41**	0.30*	0.51***	0.41**	0.15	0.15	*	
10. RCC-Spanish	0.16	0.12	0.10	0.10	0.21	0.14	0.44**	0.36*	0.37*	*

* p<0.05   ** p<0.01   *** p<0.001

communicative competence. It should also be noted that English and Spanish linguistic competence are totally unrelated (0.15) while the English and Spanish ACC are related to each other (0.51***). In other words, communicative competence appears to be an ability distinct from linguistic competence.

School 2 (bilingual elementary school)

Table 3 shows that linguistic competence in English (*BOLT*) relates positively to communicative competence in English (significantly only to RCC), while linguistic competence in Spanish (*BOLT*-Spanish) relates significantly to all the Spanish communicative competence measures. Communicative competencies do not seem to relate across languages (5/9 = 0.05, 6/10 = 0.17). Sociolinguistic competence, however, tends to correlate (3/7 = 0.56**, 4/8 = 0.28) across languages. Covert and overt speech act recognition relates highly (3/4 = 0.71**, 7/8 = 0.79**) within each language.

School 3 (monolingual elementary school)

Pupils in school 3 have almost without exception high grammatical linguistic competence in English (19.18 out of 20). Pupils did show very high variance in ACC-English despite uniform high scores on the *BOLT* (Cohen, Cruz, & Bravo, 1976) measure. Linguistic competence in Spanish (*BOLT*-Spanish) was measured for only 5 pupils. Thus no meaningful conclusions can be drawn concerning the relationship of Spanish linguistic competence to other variables. Active communicative competence in Spanish is also measured for too few individuals to permit drawing of any conclusions concerning its relation to other test scores. The data in Table 4 do suggest a relationship between sociolinguistic competence in English and ability to understand Spanish (RCC-Spanish).

School 4 (bilingual elementary school)

Linguistic competence in English (*BOLT*-English) and sociolinguistic competence (SC-overt and covert) in English and Spanish seem to interrelate but linguistic competence in Spanish (*BOLT*-Spanish) does not take part in that relationship. Receptive communicative competence did correlate across the two languages (0.58**) as shown in Table 5. Since the test of Active Communicative Competence was not administered, it was not possible to calculate this relationship across the two languages or with the measure of receptive communicative competence.

TABLE 3 *Correlations of linguistic and communicative competence measures for school 2*

Correlation measure	1	2	3	4	5	6	7	8	9	10
1. *BOLT* English	*									
2. *BOLT* Spanish	−0.34*	*								
3. SC-covert English	0.24	0.26	*							
4. SC-overt English	0.34	0.08	0.71***	*						
5. ACC-English	0.27	−0.01	0.59**	0.53**	*					
6. RCC-English	0.62**	−0.15	0.66***	0.68***	0.69***	*				
7. SC-covert Spanish	−0.15	0.74**	0.56**	0.45*	0.32	0.35	*			
8. SC-overt Spanish	0.16	0.57**	0.45**	0.28	0.15	0.47*	0.79***	*		
9. ACC-Spanish	−0.30	0.64***	−0.01	0.45	0.05	0.37	0.11**	0.73***	*	
10. RCC-Spanish	−0.10	0.43**	0.35	0.45*	0.45*	0.17	0.44**	0.19	0.35	*

* p<0.05   ** p<0.01   *** p<0.001

TABLE 4 *Correlations of linguistic and communicative competence measures for school 3*

Correlation measure	1	2	3	4	5	6	7	8	9	10
1. BOLT English	*									
2. BOLT Spanish	(0.35)	*								
3. SC-covert English	1.01	(−0.68)	*							
4. SC-overt English	0.02	(−0.76)	0.90***	*						
5. ACC-English	0.19	(0.48)	0.22	0.23	*					
6. RCC-English	0.12	(−0.38)	0.48**	0.49**	−0.12	*				
7. SC-covert Spanish	0.29	(−0.73)	0.29	0.58*	−0.22	0.75**	*			
8. SC-overt Spanish	0.42*	(−0.24)	0.47	0.55*	0.16	0.43	0.55*	*		
9. ACC-Spanish	(0.36)	(0.42)	(0.32)	(0.33)	(−0.07)	(0.05)	(−0.20)	(0.35)	*	
10. RCC-Spanish	−0.04	(0.50)	0.36*	0.34*	0.03	−0.05	−0.28	0.32	(0.44)	*

Correlations based on N <10 are placed within parentheses

* p<0.05   ** p<0.01   *** p<0.001

TABLE 5 *Correlation of linguistic and communicative competence measures for school 4*

Correlation measure	1	2	3	4	5	6	7	8
1. *BOLT* English	*	−0.01	0.31*	0.43*	0.12	0.36**	0.49**	−0.01
2. *BOLT* Spanish		*	0.14	0.04	−0.18	0.11	−0.12	−0.31*
3. SC-covert English			*	0.89***	0.43*	0.81***	0.75***	0.33*
4. SC-overt English				*	0.56***	0.77***	0.79***	0.36*
5. RCC-English					*	0.59***	0.56***	0.58*
6. SC-covert Spanish						*	0.81***	0.43*
7. SC-overt Spanish							*	0.35*
8. RCC-Spanish								*

* $p<0.05$ ** $p<0.01$ *** $p<0.001$

Several patterns emerged from the language test results of students in the three bilingual schools (school 1, 2 and 4). They were:

1. Linguistic competence in English and Spanish were negatively related;

2. Active communicative competence in English and Spanish were moderately related. (0.51***) for the high school group, but almost unrelated for school 2, the elementary group (0.05);

3. Receptive communicative competence across languages was almost unrelated in two schools (0.14 for the high school, 0.17 for elementary school — school 2) and moderately related (0.58*) in school 4;

4. Sociolinguistic competence, consisting of the recognition of overt and covert speech acts, correlated highly within English and Spanish and across the two languages in the two elementary schools;

5. Sociolinguistic competence and receptive communicative competence are related across languages in three of the schools;

6. Active communicative competence and sociolinguistic competence were moderately related within each language for the high school and bilingual elementary school (school 2).

Based on the instruments used in this study, one can conclude that linguistic competence in English and Spanish is unrelated. Knowledge of the grammatical structures of one language seems to have no association with grammatical knowledge in the other. Communicative competence in English and Spanish seems to differ according to school (age) groups. For the high school group there was a relative high correlation (0.51) between ACC-English and ACC-Spanish measures. This relationship was not found among elementary school pupils. Sociolinguistic competence, while problematic because of the item format used, did correlate across the two languages in the bilingual elementary schools, thus suggesting the presence of linguistic ability somewhat different from the active communicative measure.

Relationship of linguistic and communicative measure to achievement

To explore the relationship of linguistic and communicative proficiency to school achievement the various language measures were correlated with the number of graduation competencies passed at the end of the academic year for the high school group and with scores of the *CTBS (Comprehensive Test of Basic Skills*, McGraw-Hill, 1974) or *CAT (California Achievement Test*, Tiegs & Clark, 1970) for the three elementary schools. A summary of the results is presented by school. Table 6 presents

TABLE 6 *Relationship of language measures to school achievement*

	BOLT-English	BOLT-Spanish	SC-covert English	SC-overt English	ACC-English	RCC-English	SC-covert Spanish	SC-overt Spanish	ACC-Spanish	RCC-Spanish
School 1										
N of competencies passed	0.42*	−0.23	0.05	−0.13	0.36**	0.38*	0.04	−0.01	0.31*	0.23
School 2										
CTBS reading	0.42*	0.20	0.65**	0.58*	0.59**	0.65**	0.50*	0.46*	0.16	0.46*
CTBS language	0.43*	0.01	0.51**	0.65**	0.89	0.50*	0.38	0.29	0.94	0.37
CTBS math	0.53**	0.24	0.60**	0.41*	0.65**	0.64**	0.51**	0.52**	0.20	0.25
School 3										
CAT vocabulary	0.21	−(0.76)	0.06	0.25	0.39*	−0.01	0.43	0.40	(−0.08)	0.23
CAT read comprehension	0.24	−(0.75)	0.23	0.35	0.54***	0.94	0.63**	0.54*	(−0.06)	0.15
CAT spelling	−0.01	−(0.80)	0.24	0.32	0.01	0.16	0.19	0.59*	(−0.59)	0.27
CAT lang mech	−0.08	−(0.68)	0.43*	0.47*	0.33*	0.08	−0.10	0.24	(−0.23)	0.27
CAT expression	0.21	−(0.97)*	0.27	0.40*	0.46**	0.02	0.34	0.49*	(−0.08)	0.32
CAT math computation	−0.25	−(0.99)*	0.42*	0.44*	0.11	0.33	0.23	0.33	(−0.31)	0.43*
CAT math concepts	−0.05	−(0.96)*	0.49	0.55**	0.19	0.24	0.37	0.34	(−0.21)	0.21
CAT reference skill	0.22	−(0.94)*	0.45*	0.44*	0.32*	0.14	−9.03	0.54*	(−0.11)	0.44
School 4										
CTBS	0.11	0.32	0.31	0.41*	—	0.33	0.32	0.46*	—	0.42+

( ) Based on N 10
+   nearly significant at p<0.05
*   p<0.05
**   p<0.01
*** p<0.001

the relationships of the language measures to achievement.

For school 1, the high school, both English linguistic competence and active and passive communicative competence have a significant relation to the number of competencies achieved. Active communicative competence in Spanish is also related to this achievement measure. However, sociolinguistic competence is negatively associated with this criterion.

For school 2, the bilingual elementary school, English linguistic and communicative competence, both measured purely audio-lingually, seem to be directly related to achievement in both English reading and math. Sociolinguistic competence in both languages is also highly correlated to *CTBS* reading and math achievement. The relationship is probably due to the fact that sociolinguistic competence taps the ability to understand and interpret teachers' intentions and directions.

For school 3, monolingual elementary school, the lack of variance in English linguistic competence appears to contribute to a lack of relation with the achievement measures. The very high negative correlation between Spanish linguistic competence and school achievement indicates that, among a relatively few recent arrivals whose Spanish is very good, achievement as measured in English, is not very high. Communicative competence in English, however, has a strong relationship to most achievement measures in language arts. Again, there is a strong relationship between sociolinguistic competence and various language skills, including math achievement.

For school 4, the bilingual elementary school, sociolinguistic competence (overt) in English and Spanish were found to be related to English language skills. For these students receptive communicative competence in Spanish (L1) appears to be related to achievement in English (L2), RCC in English, measured as the ability to follow directions or instruction on school tasks, is unrelated to achievement on the *CTBS*. ACC in English and Spanish was not assessed.

The significant relationships between linguistic and communicative proficiency to school achievement for the four schools can be summarized as follows:

1. Knowledge of English grammar (linguistic competence) and the ability to understand directions (passive communicative competence) and use English functionally (active communicative competence) are related to school achievement in English among school students and pupils in elementary schools (two out of three schools).

2. Sociolinguistic competence (ability to understand and interpret communicative intentions) appears to be related to achievement

in English language skills and math in all three elementary schools.

3. Active communicative competence in Spanish is related to English achievement (number of competencies) for the high school group and receptive communicative competence in Spanish is related to English language skills and math achievement for pupils in three elementary schools.

The different patterns of relationships between the linguistic measures and achievements for the high school and elementary school population could be the result of the age (developmental) factor interacting with the achievement measure (graduation competencies — criterion tests and the *CTBS* (McGraw-Hill, 1974) or *CAT* (Tiegs & Clark, 1970) — standardized tests).

Pupil characteristics and performance on language tests

Current research on the variables affecting language assessment procedures suggest that various factors influence the test-taker's behavior and performance on tests. Carroll (1963) has noted that a positive testing experience may enhance students' willingness to persevere while a negative test experience might instill high anxiety and hamper students' perseverance and, in turn, test results. Mehan (1973) has pointed out that the elicitations procedures used during a language interview tap an interactional ability, which goes beyond a student's language proficiency. For the bilingual Hispanic student, factors such as acculturation and socialization patterns such as socio-economic status (Padilla, 1979) have been noted to affect performance on tests. Swain (1977) includes personality characteristics such as self-concept and cognitive style (field dependent/independent) as important factors affecting the learner's ability to acquire a specific feature of second language (e.g. pragmatics, grammar, and discourse).

To examine the role of a number of these factors in terms of performance on linguistic and communicative competence language measures, three variables were included in this study: (1) home language use (a type of language attitude); (2) self-concept (appraisal of oneself, particularly in relation to school life); and, (3) cognitive style (field dependent/independent based on *Group Embedded Figure Test* (Ottman, Raskins & Witkin, 1971). The results are presented in Table 7 and summarized by school.

School 1 (high school)

Home language (expressed on a scale: Spanish 3, mixed 2, English 1) had a negative relationship to English competence measures. Self-concept relates positively to all English competence measures, as well as the

TABLE 7 *Relationship of pupil characteristics (home language use, self-concept, learning style) to linguistic and communicative language measures*

	BOLT-English	BOLT-Spanish	SC-cover English	SC-oven English	ACC-English	RCC-English	SC-cover Spanish	SC-oven Spanish	ACC-Spanish	RCC-Spanish
School 1										
Home language used (Spanish)	-0.51***	0.26*	-0.24	-0.14	-0.47***	-0.44***	0.02	0.07	-0.15	0.08
Self concept	0.47***	-0.30*	0.00	0.19	0.47**	0.33**	-0.10	-0.11	0.26*	0.47*
Learning style (embedded figures test)	0.54***	0.15	0.32*	0.43*	0.50**	0.51**	0.18	0.04	0.57***	0.29*
School 2										
Home language used (Spanish)	-0.66***	0.63**	0.19	-0.28	-0.24	-0.35	0.38*	0.31	0.39*	-0.01
Self concept	-0.01	0.26	0.56*	0.54*	0.33	0.68**	0.48**	0.37	0.33	0.22
Learning style (embedded figures test)	0.19	-0.11	0.80***	0.69**	0.59**	0.55**	0.30	0.26	0.13	0.01
School 3										
Home language used (Spanish)	-0.12	(0.41)	(-9.02)	0.14	-0.24	0.23	-0.36	-0.25	(0.85**)	0.26
Self concept	-0.15	(-9.50)	0.71**	0.76**	0.01	0.05	(0.15)	(0.12)	(0.33)	0.60
Learning style (embedded figures test)	-0.24	(1.00)	-0.18	-0.06	0.01	-0.41	(-0.37)	(-0.58)	(0.88*)	0.25
School 4										
Self concept	0.41*	-0.23+	0.49**	0.58**	—	0.23	0.36**	0.41**	—	0.17
Learning style (embedded figures test)	0.23	-0.29+	0.46**	0.46***	—	0.47**	0.50**	0.59***	—	0.31

( ) Based on N = 10
+ Nearly significant at p<0.05
* p<0.05
** p<0.01
*** p<0.001

Spanish communicative competence, but has a negative relation to Spanish linguistic competence. Field independence tends to be positively related to all the chief measures of language competence, including the communicative competence in English as well as Spanish. Evidently, communicative competence as measured and conceptualized in the tests devised (information giving ability) relates also to an analytic (field independent) learning style.

School 2 (bilingual elementary school)

Quite expectedly, home language (Spanish) relates positively with Spanish and negatively with English linguistic competence. Self concept has no strong relation to either linguistic competencies, but relates significantly to communicative competence in English as well as Spanish. Field independent learning style has positive relations to all the communicative competence measures of English, including sociolinguistic competence.

School 3 (monolingual elementary school)

Home language is related to active communicative competence in Spanish. Sociolinguistic competence in English has a positive relation to pupil's self-concept. In spite of the uniformly high linguistic competence in English, pupils in School 3 show very high variance in active English communicative competence. However, unlike in the case of School 1 and 2 pupils, communicative competence in English shows no relation to field independent learning style. It is possible that the fact that School 3 pupils are not in the process of learning English as a second language in a school setting may account for this difference.

School 4 (bilingual elementary school)

Linguistic competence in English and sociolinguistic competence in both English and Spanish have positive correlations with self-concept. Sociolinguistic competence and receptive communicative competence in both languages is related to a field independent learning style.

The results obtained from this analysis suggest the following relationships:

1. Home language (Spanish) has a negative relation to English language measures and a positive association with Spanish linguistic competence in three schools and Spanish communicative competence in two elementary schools.

2. Self-concept relates positively to communicative competence in both languages and to linguistic in English in Schools 1 and 2. Sociolinguistic competence is also associated with a positive self-concept in Schools 3 and 4.

3. Field independent learning style is related to both English linguistic competence and communicative competence at the high school level.

4. Field independent learning style is primarily associated with communicative measures at the elementary school level.

Performance on both linguistic and communicative competence tests, as a result of home language use, self-concept, and a field independent learning style, appear to be influenced by the age/grade factor. High school students who are field dependent do not perform well on either linguistic or communicative competence tests. The communicative competence measures developed for this study favor field independent learners. A positive self-concept results in a higher communicative proficiency in both languages and sociolinguistic competence. One can speculate that the student with a positive attitude about himself/herself may be more willing to perform language tasks that have a communicative dimension.

Implications for the measurement of communicative proficiency

The results of the research findings reviewed here suggest that communicative proficiency (receptive and productive) can be assessed with a discrete-point instrument. Various dimensions of communicative proficiency (ability to convey information accurately, interpret communicative intention, and follow directions) can be included in a test which exhibits relatively high reliability. By emphasizing the communicative functions of school language (transmitting information accurately, following directions on school tasks, and understanding the communicative intentions of classroom language), it is possible to develop an instrument that relates to school achievement.

A number of important issues remain to be addressed. By conceptualizing communicative proficiency primarily in terms of school-related language, one may underestimate a speaker's range of mastery. The use of separate tests for each language may not capture the full repertoire of the bilingual speaker, who may often code-switch while performing various communicative acts. In addition, communicative proficiency could vary depending on a number of contextual factors including such aspects as setting, topic, and addressee. Beyond these sociolinguistic factors, performance on the communicative measures used here appear to be affected by such pupil characteristics as age (secondary vs. elementary school) and learning style. A field independent learning style and a positive self-concept produce better results on these communicative measures. The development of a communicative proficiency instrument that is both sensitive to developmental factors and acculturation aspects involved in test-taking presents an important challenge.

APPENDIX A

Sample of items and scoring procedures for
Active Communicative Competence Test

book		bird
lying flat		on ball
face down		facing left
title — *Star Wars*		eye
title on spine		feathers
title upside down		4 or 5 feathers
pages		beak
ball		legs
on book		toes
lines on ball/basketball		3 toes per foot
5 lines on ball (or just "basketball")		whistling/singing/lines

Section 1.A.1 Drawing pictures
(Sit opposite the child. Do not let him/her see what you are drawing.)

I am going to show you a picture. There are three pictures and I don't know
which one is on top. Describe it to me very carefully so that I can draw the picture
from your description. Tell me *what* things to draw, *how many* things there are,
where to draw them, and tell me if something is happening in the picture. I will
draw only what you say, so tell me how to put them in the right place so that the
picture comes out looking exactly like this (*point to picture*).

APPENDIX B

Sample of items and scoring procedures for
Receptive Communicative Competence Test

Whoever first said "as slow as molasses
in January" was a genius of sorts. Molasses, a thick, dark
syrup, becomes almost impossible to pour when it is cold.
Anything or anyone that moves as slowly as molasses in
January moves very slow indeed.

3.

4.

5.

1. Underline all the words which begin with capital letters.
2. In the second line of the paragraph, put circles around the words which are between commas.
3. Next to the number three (3) on your paper, write the word that is immediately before and the word that is immediately after the quotation marks.
4. Next to the number four (4) on your paper, write the word that appears twice on line four (4) of the paragraph.
5. Next to the number five (5) on your paper, write the name of the month which comes before and the name of the month which comes after the one mentioned in this paragraph.

C. Paragraph
☐ (1) Underlined: *Whoever, January, Molasses, Anything, January* (complete word must be underlined)
    (2) Circled: ☐ (4) Line 4 — as
       a   (5) Line 5 —
☐   thick   ☐   December
☐   dark   ☐   February
☐ (3) Line 3 —
☐   said   POSSIBLE: 11
☐   as   TOTAL SCORE: ——————
☐   January
☐   was

APPENDIX C

Sample item of Sociolinguistic Competence Test

1. John was working on his math problems and his teacher, Miss Jones, wanted to know if he needed any help. What are *two* ways that she could say this?

   A. How are you?
   B. How are you doing?
   C. Isn't this homework easy?
   D. Do you need help?

2. The students were making noise in the history class. The teacher wanted them to be quiet. What are *two* ways that he could say this?

   A. What's the noise all about?
   B. Be quiet.
   C. You're talking together.
   D. Let's be careful.

Note

1. The research reported in this article was performed as part of a project funded by the National Institute of Education, Department of Education (NIE-G-79-0130). Some of the results of this study have been reported elsewhere, see Politzer, Shohamy & McGroarty 1981 and Politzer & Ramírez, 1981. The opinions expressed in this publication do not reflect the position, policy, or endorsement of the National Institute of Education.

References

Arias, M. B. 1976, *A bicultural approach to the issue of self concept assessment.* Unpublished doctoral dissertation, University of California at Stanford.

Austin, J. 1962, *How to do things with words.* London: Oxford University Press.

Briere, E. 1971, Are we really measuring proficiency with our language tests? *Foreign Language Annals*, 4, 385–91.

—— 1979, Testing communicative language proficiency. In R. Silverstein (ed.), *Occasional Papers on Linguistics #6: Proceedings of the Third International Conference on Frontiers in Language Proficiency Testing.* Carbondale, Illinois: Southern Illinois University, 254–75.

Canale, M. & Swain, M. 1980, Theoretical basis of communicative approaches to second language teaching and testing. *Applied linguistics,* 1(1), 1–7.

Carroll, J. B. 1963, A model of school learning. *Teachers College Record,* 64, 723–33.

Cohen, S., Cruz, R. & Bravo, R. 1976, *Bahia Oral Language Test.* Berkeley, CA: Bahia, Inc.

Coopersmith, E. 1967, *The antecedents of self-esteem.* San Francisco: Freeman.

Corrigan, A. & Upshur, J. A. 1978, *Test method and linguistic factors in foreign language tests.* Paper presented at the TESOL Convention, Mexico City.

CTBS/McGraw-Hill 1974, *Comprehensive Tests of Basic Skills (CTBS) — Levels A-C, 1 and 2, Form S*. Monterey, CA: Author.

Davies, A. 1978, Language testing. *Language Teaching and Linguistics Abstracts*, 11, 145–59; 215–31.

Dulay, H. & Burt, M. 1980, The relative proficiency of limited English proficiency students. *NABE Journal*, 4(3), 1–24.

Duncan, S. E. & De Avila, E. A. 1979, Bilingualism and cognition: Some recent findings. *NABE Journal*, 4(1), 15–30.

Flavell, J. & Botkin, P. T., *et al.* 1968, *The development of role-taking and communication skills in children*. New York: John Wiley, Inc.

Hymes, D. 1971, Competence and performance in linguistic theory. In B. Huxley & E. Ingram (eds), *Language acquisition: Models and methods*. London: Academic Press.

John-Steiner, V. P. 1979, Osterreich, Helga and Nihlen, Ann: The evaluation of communicative competence in bilingual children. *Bilingual Resources*, 2(2), 11–14.

Legaretta, D. 1979, The effects of program models on language acquisition by Spanish speaking children. *TESOL Quarterly*, 13(4), 521–34.

Mehan, H. 1973, Assessing children's language using abilities: Methodologic and cross cultural implications. In M. Armer & A. D. Grimshaw (eds), *Comparative social research: Methodologic problems and strategies*. New York: John Wiley, Inc.

Morrow, D. 1977, *Techniques of evaluation for a notional syllabus*. London: Royal Society of Arts.

Ottman, P. K., Raskins, E. & Witkin, H. A. 1971, *Group embedded figure test*. Palo Alto, CA: Consulting Psychologists Press.

Padilla, A. M. 1979, Critical factors in the testing of Hispanic Americans: A review and some suggestions for the future. In *Testing, teaching and learning: A report of a conference on research on testing*. Washington, D.C.: National Institute of Education.

Politzer, R. L., Shohamy, E. & McGroarty, M. 1981, *Validation of linguistic and communicative oral language tests for Spanish-English bilingual pupils*. Paper presented at the TESOL Colloquium on Validation of Oral Proficiency Tests. Ann Arbor, Michigan. March.

Politzer, R. L. & Ramírez, A. G. 1981, Linguistic and communicative competence of students in a Spanish/English bilingual high school program. *NABE Journal*, 5(3), 81–104.

Ramírez, M. & Castañeda. A. 1974 *Cultural democracy: Bicognitive development and education*. New York: Academic Press.

Rosansky, E. J. 1980, Research efforts in the development of multiple indicators of communicative competence and effects of bilingual education. In J. E. Alatis (ed.), *Georgetown University Round Table on Languages and Linguistics*. Washington, D.C.: Georgetown University Press.

Savignon, S. J. 1972, *Communicative competence: An experiment in foreign language teaching*. Philadelphia, PA: Center for Curriculum Development.

Searle, J. 1969, *Speech Acts: An essay in the philosophy of language*. London: Cambridge University Press.

Shuy, R. W. 1979, On the relevance of recent developments in sociolinguistics to the study of language learning and early education. *NABE Journal*, 6, 51-72.

Stevenson, D. K. 1979, *Beyond faith and face validity: The multitrait-multimethod matrix and the convergent and discriminant validity of oral proficiency tests.* Paper presented at the TESOL Convention, Boston, MA.

Swain, M. 1977, Future directions in second language research. In C. A. Henning (ed.), *Proceedings of the Los Angeles Second Language Research Forum.* Los Angeles: University of California at Los Angeles.

Tiegs, E. W. & Clark, W. W. 1970, *California Achievement Tests (CAT) — Levels II and III, Form A.* Monterey, CA: CTB/McGraw-Hill.

Wang, M., Rose, S. & Marwell, J. 1973, *The development of the language communication skill tasks.* Pittsburgh: Learning and Research and Development Center.

Wiemann, J. & Backlund, P. 1980, Current theory and research in communicative competence. *Review of Educational Research,* 1(50), 185–200.

Witkin, H. A., Ottman, P. H. K., Raskin, E. & Karp, S. A. 1971, *A manual for the embedded figures test.* Palo Alto: Consulting Psychologist Press.

Zirkel, P. A. 1971, Self concept and the "disadvantage" of ethnic group membership and mixture. *Review of Educational Research,* 41, 211–25.

A communicative approach to language proficiency assessment in a minority setting

Michael Canale
The Ontario Institute for Studies in Education

Beginning with Carroll (1961), there has been a growing trend in the language testing field to consider the assessment of language proficiency from the perspective of language use and communication, that is, with the focus less on knowledge of discrete grammatical forms and more on overall skill in using language for natural purposes in realistic situations. This trend, which Spolsky (1978) labels the "integrative-sociolinguistic" one, owes a large part of its current popularity and substance to modern sociolinguistics, particularly to the work of Hymes (1967; 1968; 1972) on the ethnography of speaking and on the notion of communicative competence.

The major argument for this communication-oriented approach to language proficiency assessment has to do with instrument (or test) validity. It is commonly claimed that communication-oriented instruments may possess both higher internal (construct and content) validity and higher external (face) validity than do more grammar-oriented instruments (for example, see Carroll, 1961; Morrow, 1977). However, there are two important questions that must be raised with respect to the validity of communication-oriented language proficiency instruments. The first concerns construct, content and face validity: In view of the confusion and disagreement over the definitions of communication and communicative competence (cf. Canale & Swain, 1980), just what are the specifications for test content and format that must be satisfied for an instrument to qualify as communication-oriented? The second question, suggested by Cummins (in press), addresses predictive validity: Since increasing use is made of language proficiency tests (of whatever orientation) for admission, placement and exit purposes in academic programs, what is the relationship between communicative proficiency in a given language and achievement in an academic program taught in this language? Cummins' own view is that the relationship is questionable; and he states:

"Many linguists, influenced no doubt by the naïve assumptions regarding these relationships made by practitioners of compensatory education, have argued that language proficiency can be validly assessed only in naturally-occurring communicative contexts. Linguistic manipulation, or CALP (cognitive/academic language proficiency) tasks are thus regarded as inappropriate to assess language proficiency. This approach, however, ignores the more academically-relevant aspects of language proficiency and amounts to identifying language proficiency with BICS (basis interpersonal communicative skill). It is thus likely to result in inaccurate placement decisions." (in press, pp. 26–27)

Thus, the two questions raised here have to do with the nature of communicative proficiency and its relevance to academic achievement. Obviously, a response to the first question is required before the second question can be addressed in a direct manner.

The purpose of the present paper is to outline a language proficiency assessment project at O.I.S.E. (begun in May 1981) that offers an opportunity to respond to the above questions in the context of a language minority setting, that of the Franco-Ontarians — the French-speaking population of Ontario. Section 1 below presents a brief description of the Franco-Ontarian minority situation and identifies the educational needs that the project is to address. Sections 2 and 3 present a discussion of the communicative approach the project has adopted and the nature of the assessment instruments to be developed. Finally, the criteria that the instruments must satisfy and the research issues that are raised, are examined in Section 4.

Project background

The Franco-Ontarian minority situation

Although both French and English were recognized as Canada's official languages in the (1867) British North America Act (Ollivier, 1962) only in the province of Quebec do speakers of French-as-a-mother-tongue constitute a majority. Of the approximately one million French-speaking Canadians who live outside of Quebec, the largest concentration (462,190 according to the 1976 Census of Canada) is in Ontario. The Franco-Ontarian situation is an extremely unstable one: French-speakers make up less than 7% of the population of Ontario; French is not recognized as an official language under provincial legislation; public schooling in French (at the elementary and secondary levels) was legislated only in 1968; in this same year, the Ontario Government adopted the policy of providing other public services (e.g. court hearings) in French, where *feasible;* the majority of Franco-Ontarians are in the lowest socio-economic class; French-language media are limited; French is not the language of the working place in the majority of jobs; and approximately half of the Ontarians of French origin report English as the dominant language used in the home (cf. Mougeon, 1980; Mougeon & Canale, 1979).

The communicative proficiency assessment project

This project, directed by Professor Raymond Mougeon (OISE) and Professor Michael Canale, has received funding for an initial period of one year through the Franco-Ontarian Centre at O.I.S.E. The goal of the project is to develop, with the assistance of Franco-Ontarian educators, two communicative proficiency instruments for use in French-language schools in Ontario at the end of Grade 8: one instrument for French as a first language and another for English as a second language. These instruments are intended to serve the needs of Franco-Ontarian educators in three major ways:

1. Evaluation of Language Arts programs in the elementary grades is an important concern in view of the newly released curriculum guidelines for Français (French as a first language) and Anglais (English as a second language) from the Ontario Ministry of Education. These guidelines explicitly emphasize the use of French and English for communication as central program aims. One valuable means of assessing how well the proposed curriculum — and programs — actually work toward these aims is to provide an independent (unrelated to specific programs) assessment of the communicative proficiency of students who participate in these programs. The instruments that the project develops can be an important component of this independent assessment, given the lack of suitable instruments at present.

2. There is need for instruments for use in decisions about admission to and placement in French-language secondary schools and Language Arts programs at the secondary level. For example, Franco-Ontarian educators must make decisions on the placement in Language Arts and other programs of students who have

received their elementary education in French-language schools within the same board of education as the secondary school, students from other boards of education (within and outside of Ontario), and students who have acquired French-language skills in English-language schools (e.g. via French immersion programs; cf. Swain, 1978). Lack of suitable proficiency assessment instruments often leads these educators to base their decisions on assessment which is neither systematic nor objective (cf. Cazabon & Frenette, 1980) or on results from administration of instruments chosen according to inadequate criteria such as cost, ease of administration, popularity, and ease of access (as discussed by Bernal, 1979).

3. The development of communicative proficiency instruments for both French and English should allow Franco-Ontarian educators and other researchers to confront the dangerous bias in instrument use and interpretation of results that has been documented for Franco-Ontarian students and other language-minority groups in Canada (cf. Canale & Mougeon, 1978). For example, an article in *The Globe and Mail* (October 4, 1977, p. 4) — Canada's "national" newspaper — implied that Franco-Ontarian students are "semi-lingual," having no adequate proficiency in French or English, and reported that their French is bastardized and unsystematic, making it difficult for them to express themselves clearly and to understand one another. As revealed in the study by Cazabon & Frenette (1980), such a viewpoint is a source of great anxiety for Language Arts teachers and other Franco-Ontarian educators. Since this viewpoint is based on both prejudice and the (mis)use of instruments that measure essentially mastery of standard (French and English) grammar, it is important that more communication-oriented assessment of these students be available and encouraged.

A communicative approach to proficiency assessment

As pointed out in the introduction to this paper, one of the basic concerns of a communicative approach to language proficiency assessment must be the nature of communication and communicative competence. To the extent that these notions are undefined or inadequately defined, instrument validation procedures become less persuasive and the label "communicative" becomes more vacuous and gratuitous. An adequate description of these notions is crucial not only to instrument content — that is, what is to be assessed — but also to instrument format or method — that is, how proficiency is to be assessed. The concern here, then, is mainly with construct validity which is assumed to be a function of both instrument content and format (cf. Bachman & Palmer, 1981a, 1981b for further discussion).

This concern with the nature of communication and communicative competence was addressed in the context of another project, The Ontario Assessment Instrument Pool for French as a Second Language Project. The view of communication adopted on that project is that proposed by Morrow (1977). There he proposed seven features of communication which have been reformulated in Canale (1981) and Canale & Swain (1980) as follows: communication

1. is interaction-based in that communication skills are normally both acquired and used in social interaction;
2. involves unpredictability and creativity in both form and message;
3. takes place in discourse and sociocultural contexts which provide constraints on appropriate language use and also clues as to correct interpretations of utterances;
4. is carried out under limiting psychological and other conditions such as memory constraints, fatigue, and distractions;
5. always has a purpose (for example, to establish social relations, to persuade, or to promise);
6. involves authentic as opposed to textbook-contrived language; and
7. is judged as successful or not on the basis of actual outcomes. (For example, communication could be judged successful in the case of a non-native English speaker who was trying to find the train station in Washington, uttered the ungrammatical sentence "How to go train?" to a passer-by, and was given directions to the train station.)

In addition, communication is understood in our work as the exchange and negotiation of information between at least two individuals through the use of verbal and nonverbal symbols, oral and written/visual modes, and production and comprehension processes. Information is assumed to consist of conceptual, sociocultural, affective, and other content as discussed in Hymes (1972) and elsewhere. Furthermore, such information is never permanently worked out nor fixed at any level of content but is constantly changing and qualified by such factors as preceding and further information, context of communication, choice of language forms, and nonverbal behavior. Of course, this characterization of communication is not exhaustive; it and the view of communicative competence outlined below are intended only as the *minimum* characterization adequate for the research program at O.I.S.E. concerned with beginning students in general second language programs in Ontario. For further discussion of this notion of communication, see Canale (1981), Canale (in press), and Canale & Swain (1980).

The view of communicative competence adopted on the earlier project is that proposed in Canale & Swain (1980) and extended in Canale (1981). This theoretical framework minimally includes four areas of knowledge and skill, sketched below.

1. *Grammatical competence:* mastery of the language code (verbal or nonverbal), thus concerned with such features as lexical items and rules of sentence formation, pronunciation, and literal meaning.

2. *Sociolinguistic competence:* mastery of appropriate language use in different sociolinguistic contexts, with emphasis on appropriateness of meanings (e.g. attitudes, speech acts, and propositions) and appropriateness of forms (e.g. register, nonverbal expression, and intonation).

3. *Discourse competence:* mastery of how to combine and interpret forms and meanings to achieve a unified spoken or written text in different genres by using (a) cohesion devices to relate utterance forms (e.g. pronouns, transition words, and parallel structures) and (b) coherence rules to organize meanings (e.g. repetition, progression, consistency, and relevance of ideas).

4. *Strategic competence:* mastery of verbal and nonverbal strategies (a) to compensate for breakdowns in communication due to insufficient competence or to performance limitations (e.g. strategies such as use of dictionaries, paraphrase, and gestures) and (b) to enhance the effectiveness of communication (e.g. deliberately slow and soft speech for rhetorical effect).

It is assumed that this theory of communicative competence interacts with other systems of knowledge and skills (e.g. world knowledge, general perception strategies) as well as with a theory of human action (dealing with such factors as volition and personality). Although this theoretical framework is based on a broad range of research and does serve to identify the general content and boundaries of communicative competence, it is inadequate in important ways. For example, there is little evidence for its correctness; it is not known whether certain of its components are more or less crucial than others at various stages of first and second language acquisition; and little of substance can be said of the manner in which these components interact at different stages of language acquisition (cf. Canale & Swain, 1980; Canale, 1981 for further discussion).

In spite of such inadequacies, this notion of communicative competence and the characterization of communication outlined above have proven useful in suggesting specifications for content, formats and scoring criteria in communication-oriented language proficiency assessment (cf. Canale, 1981; Canale & Swain, 1981; Wesche, 1981; Bachman & Palmer, 1981b). Some of these specifications are presented in Section 3 below. Before turning to them, however, it is worthwhile to make explicit two key assumptions that guided instrument development on the earlier project at O.I.S.E., two assumptions which take on special significance in the context of the new project described here. They are based directly on recent work in sociolinguistics and the ethnography of speaking: (1) the principle of variability, i.e. that language use in a given community is not (normally) based on a single homogeneous set of rules at the linguistic, sociolinguistic, discourse and strategic levels but rather reflects a variety of such systems whose use is sensitive to aspects of socio-cultural and discourse contexts; and (2) the view that nonstandard language varieties are nonetheless authentic and socially-valuable linguistic systems. These assumptions are based primarily on the pioneering work of Hymes (1968) and Labov (1969; 1972). The relevance of these assumptions to the Franco-Ontarian minority situation has been stressed in Canale & Mougeon (1978). There it was pointed out that not only is the language and culture of Franco-Ontarians different from those of other francophone groups but also there is systematic linguistic variation according to regional, socio-economic and stylistic factors. Such differences and variation must, it was argued, be considered in the selection and development of language assessment instruments, along with the interpretation of results, when dealing with language minority groups such as the Franco-Ontarians.

Design of the communicative proficiency assessment instruments

The focus in this section is on the suggested components and scoring procedures for the instruments the project is to develop. These specifications are for the moment general enough so as to apply to both the French-language instrument and the English-language one; however, differences in specifications for the instruments are likely to emerge as these suggestions are subjected to further thought and feedback. These initial specifications are based mainly on three sources: (1) the assumptions and framework discussed briefly in Section 2; (2) descriptions of actual language use (English and French) among Franco-Ontarians (e.g. study by

Mougeon, 1980); and (3) feedback from Franco-Ontarian educators on the academic and social needs of students (e.g. through formal channels such as curriculum guidelines from the Ontario Ministry of Education and surveys, and through informal channels such as experience and personal communication with educators). In addition, helpful suggestions for assessment techniques and scoring procedures have been found in the work of B. J. Carroll (1980), Clark (1980), Cziko (1981), Farhady (1980), Fishman & Cooper (1978), Hinofotis (1981), Jones (1977, 1979), Lado (1978), Morrow (1977) and Pike (1973).

Suggested components

Each instrument is to contain five components, described briefly as follows.

1. *Listening comprehension.* This section will consist of several short passages — or mini-dialogues, recorded audio-visually and each of about three minutes duration. These mini-dialogues will vary according to situational factors such as topic, number and roles of participants, purpose, setting, attitudes, language varieties, rate of speech, and complexity and familiarity of ideas. These social and academic situations will be as authentic as possible, and students will respond to open-ended questions (at least at the piloting stage) demanding understanding and recall of factual information as well as judgements as to purposes, participants' roles, attitudes, probable outcomes, etc. In striving for authenticity, it is likely that certain utterances in the mini-dialogues will contain flaws (e.g. in grammar, in discourse coherence); thus students will have the opportunity to demonstrate how well they can cope with performance limitations by relying on communication strategies (e.g. visual input) and on grammatical, sociolinguistic and discourse cues.

2. *Reading comprehension.* This section will be composed of two types of tasks: a series of short passages (about 300 words each) and a longer passage (of about 1000 words). The short passages will vary mainly according to type of text and subject matter; for example, tasks might involve understanding of instructions, labels, advertisements, telegrams, school and job forms, newspaper articles, math problems, and bus schedules. The longer passage will be from a social science textbook for use in Grade 9 (or slightly above the Grade 8 level). It will be selected so as to introduce new information and new/infrequent vocabulary and will be accompanied by a set of dictionary entries for some of this

vocabulary. The purpose of this longer passage is to allow students to demonstrate their ability to cope with new information in a lengthy text and to make use of a dictionary and contextual cues to grasp the meanings of new words. For both sets of texts, students will respond to open-ended questions (again, at least at the piloting stage) requiring understanding of factual, sociolinguistic and attitudinal information.

3. *Oral interaction.* This component is designed to give the student a chance to use the language in various face-to-face situations. An oral-interview format consisting of four parts will be used. One part will be devoted to discussion of the student's background, current interests, and aspirations; a second, to role-playing in different situations for different purposes; a third, to detailed description of an object or process presented visually; and the final part will be a listing of the names of objects and persons related to a common theme (e.g. listing of 20 objects presented in a picture of a classroom). Scoring criteria, discussed briefly below, would in each part consider both formal linguistic and other communication-oriented aspects of student performance.

4. *Written expression.* This component contains two parts: an editing task and an essay, each of about 500 words. The editing task will consist of a draft essay presenting a viewpoint on a familiar topic; the student's task will be to edit the essay, that is to detect and correct errors in both usage (e.g. sentence structure, vocabulary, punctuation, spelling) and use (e.g. sociolinguistic appropriateness and discourse cohesion). The second task will be the write-up of a comparison of viewpoints on a contemporary issue; the issue and alternative viewpoints will be first discussed orally by the students and examiner to help generate ideas. As in the above section involving oral interaction, scoring criteria would be selected so as to focus on both formal linguistic and other aspects of written expression. Holistic (or global) scoring will also be attempted at the piloting stage.

5. *Self-evaluation questionnaire.* This questionnaire will allow students both to describe in scalar-fashion and to comment on their attitudes toward the language, language use habits, and perceived strengths and weaknesses in communication. Questions will bear, for example, on different language varieties, different communication modes (e.g. oral interaction, reading comprehension) and different competence areas (e.g. grammatical, sociolinguistic). The questionnaire is designed not only for the opportunity it

provides the student to reflect on his or her communication skills and preferences but also for the information it may provide Franco-Ontarian educators about student attitudes and motivation.

Scoring procedures

Considerations regarding scoring procedures for the two instruments fall into several areas: scoring criteria; the number, variety and training of scorers; the weighting of criteria; and the practicality of scoring procedures. Some comments on reliability and practicality of scoring follow in Section 4. Five criteria will be briefly described that have been developed on the Ontario Assessment Instrument Pool, French as a Second Language Project at O.I.S.E. for scoring lengthy open-ended responses on tasks requiring oral or written expression (see also Canale, 1981).

1. *Information.* Important here are the amount, relevance, clarity and factual correctness of information communicated by the student.

2. *Grammaticality.* This criterion deals with the (grammatical) correctness of vocabulary usage, word formation and sentence formation. A distinction is made between major errors — which present major obstacles to communication — and minor errors — which involve only minor disturbances of communication. In general, major errors involve sentence formation and "content" words (e.g. nouns and verbs) while minor errors involve word formation and "grammatical function" words (e.g. prepositions and relative pronouns).

3. *Pronunciation/spelling.* For oral responses this refers to the correctness of word pronunciation, liaison, word stress and sentence/ phrase intonation. For written responses it includes correctness in spelling (including accents, if applicable), use of hyphens in compound words, and use of punctuation.

4. *Appropriateness.* The concern here is the extent to which both the information and form of information are socially appropriate and natural/authentic (e.g. appropriate degree of politeness and formality, most likely form of message that native-speakers would use) depending on such contextual variables as topic, role of participants, setting and purpose.

5. *Discourse.* This involves the extent to which utterances function together to form a unified (spoken or written) text. Attention is paid to both cohesion in form (i.e. use of transition words such as *then, however;* use of pronouns and synonyms; and repetition of

key words and sentence patterns) and coherence in thought (i.e. development of ideas, organization, and consistency of viewpoint).

The criteria Grammaticality, Appropriateness and Discourse are meant to reflect directly the theory of communicative competence discussed in Section 2 above. Pronunciation/spelling are not included in the description for Grammaticality since such criteria have been found to be poor predictors of grammatical (and other) skills (e.g. Wilds, 1975). The criterion Information is intended as an overall consequence of world knowledge and grammatical, sociolinguistic and discourse competence, with focus on strategic competence in particular. Canale (1981) and McLean (1980) discuss data gathered by the Ontario Assessment Instrument Pool, French as a Second Language Project at O.I.S.E. which offer tentative support for distinguishing these five criteria. Additional criteria may be desirable; for example, Hinofotis (1981), Lepicq (1980) and Wiemann & Backlund (1980) draw attention to the role of affective variables – such as confidence and willingness to communicate — in contributing to effective communication in both academic and non-academic settings.

Concluding remarks

This concluding section is limited to a few short comments on the characteristics that the two communicative proficiency instruments should possess, how these characteristics might be attained, and what research issues can be addressed through this project.

Instrument characteristics

There are five criteria that are to guide the development of the two proficiency instruments.

1. *Validity*. The concern here is not only whether the instruments measure what they are intended to measure but also whether what they measure is relevant to success in academic programs in a language minority setting. The first concern will be addressed both judgementally (as to content and face validity — cf. Clark, 1978) and more objectively through use of criterion instruments, as described in Clark (1980). The second concern will be handled as one of predictive validity; hence correlations with academic achievement will be examined for the different components of each instrument. Construct validity checks — for example,

through procedures such as the multi-trait, multi-method conver-
gent-discriminant design discussed by Bachman & Palmer (1981a,
1981b) — are being considered.

2. *Reliability.* The concern raised by this criterion is with factors that
may reduce the consistency — or reliability — of results: e.g.
order of presentation of items; administration procedures; scoring
procedures; and item content and format. To increase reliability,
different forms of instruments will be developed and pilot-tested,
and both objective and judgemental feedback will be considered
in instrument analysis.

3. *Practicality.* Time and cost of instrument administration and
scoring are important here. While factors such as ease of access,
ease of administration and ease of scoring are inadequate criteria
on which to base instrument selection, they are desirable characteristics. To this end, it is likely that the actual instruments can be
administered in no more than two hours and that certain items be
scorable by machine (e.g. multiple-choice formats in the reading
comprehension and listening comprehension components) and
others by rapid, impressionistic (holistic) procedures (e.g. certain
parts of the oral interaction and written expression components).

4. *Acceptability.* This criterion, as discussed by B. J. Carroll (1980),
involves the willingness/motivation of both educators and students
to use the instrument in question. In work at O.I.S.E. on the
Ontario Assessment Instrument Pool, French as a Second Language Project, we have observed that innovations in instrument
content and format can be a source of confusion and resistance
among educators. Shohamy & Jorstod (1980) report on the
negative attitudes of students toward cloze tests and positive ones
toward the interview format of the Foreign Service Institute's
Oral Interview; such attitudes may influence student performance
on instruments. Our project will address this criterion by involving educators in instrument development, soliciting subjective
feedback on instruments from both educators and students, and
selecting items that are authentic and relevant in both content and
format.

5. *Feedback potential.* Here the focus is on not only how results are
reported to educators and students but also the learning experience that is offered to the students and perceived by educators.
For example, results must be reported to educators and decision-
makers so as to have clear application to the questions and
problems to be addressed. Also, Clark (1972) and Jones (1981)

have argued that indirect assessment procedures cannot have the same psychological and instructional impact as do direct ones involving more authentic and meaningful communicative interaction. The involvement of educators on the project will be valuable for assuring proper reporting procedures, and the inclusion of direct assessment procedures (e.g. in oral interaction and written expression) as well as the variety of content, modes and testing formats, are helpful to increase the potential learning experience for students.

In addition to addressing the needs of Franco-Ontarian educators as sketched in Section 1, this project allows us to deal with several important research issues in the area of language proficiency assessment in a language minority situation. Four such issues are summarized here.

1. The project will gather data bearing on the degree of correctness of the theoretical framework for communicative competence outlined in Section 2 and, indirectly, on assumptions and hypotheses that are important in recent work in sociolinguistics and ethnography. In this light, the two instruments to be developed are seen as research tools and experiments in themselves.

2. Project findings will bear on the question of the relevance of communicative proficiency — as described in this paper — to academic achievement in a language minority setting. For example, Pike (1973) has stressed that TOEFL scores, and language proficiency in general, should not be expected to correlate highly with Grade Point Average; Oller (1979) has argued that language proficiency is indistinguishable from general intellectual skills and academic achievement; and Cummins (in press) argues that only one aspect of language proficiency — CALP (cognitive/academic language proficiency) but not BICS (basic interpersonal communicative skills) — is highly related to academic achievement. Of interest also is the view cited by Oller & Spolsky (1979) that language proficiency is not necessarily constant and may thus change over relatively short periods of time.

3. A related issue is that of the nature of language proficiency: To what extent is it a unitary, global construct (as argued by Oller, 1979) and to what extent is it better characterized in the manner proposed by Cummins (in press) as including both a CALP and BICS component?

4. Finally, what is the relationship between first-language proficiency and second-language proficiency in a language minority setting? A popular view in the Franco-Ontarian setting (and else-

where — cf. Canale & Mougeon, 1978) is that young Franco-Ontarians are "semilingual" in both French and English. Cummins (in press) argues that for language minority members, first and second language CALP may be interdependent but that no such relationship seems to exist in the case of BICS.

The questions raised here are difficult ones, and the project described has set itself very ambitious goals. However, the domain of language proficiency assessment in a language minority setting is a complex one that is unlikely to benefit from formulating simple questions and simple ways to respond to them. To paraphrase Einstein, we must try to make our questions and goals as simple as possible, but no simpler.

References

Bachman, L. & Palmer, A. S. 1981a, The construct validation of the Foreign Service Institute (FSI) oral interview. *Language Learning*, 31(1), 67–86.
—— 1981b, *The construct validation of tests of communicative competence.* Paper presented at the Colloquium on the Validation of Oral Proficiency Tests, University of Michigan, March.
Bernal, E. M., Jr. 1979, What makes language test an expletive: Tests, test selection, and test use. In C. A. Yorio, K. Perkins & J. Schachter (eds), *On TESOL '79: The learner in focus.* Washington, D.C.: TESOL.
Canale, M. 1981, Introduction to the Ontario Assessment Instrument Pool for French as a second language. In *The Ontario Assessment Instrument Pool for French as a Second Language.* Toronto: Ontario Ministry of Education.
—— 1981b, From communicative competence to communicative language pedagogy. In J. C. Richards & R. Schmidt (eds.), *Language and communication.* Book in preparation.
—— in press, On some dimensions of language proficiency. In J. W. Oller, Jr. (ed.), *Current issues in language testing research.* Rowley, Mass.: Newbury House.
Canale, M. & Mougeon, R. 1978, Problèmes posés par la mesure du rendement en français des élèves franco-ontariens. In B. Cazabon (ed.), *Langue maternelle, langue première de communication?* Sudbury, Ontario: Institut franco-ontarien. Also published in *Working Papers on Bilingualism*, 16, 92–110.
Canale, M. & Swain, M. 1980, Theoretical bases of communicative approaches to second language teaching and testing. *Applied Linguistics*, 1(1), 1–47.
—— 1981, A domain description for core French as a second language (FSL): Communication skills. In *The Ontario Assessment Instrument Pool for French as a Second Language.* Toronto: Ontario Ministry of Education.
Carroll, B. J. 1980, *Testing communicative performance.* Oxford: Pergamon Press.
Carroll, J. B. 1961, Fundamental considerations in testing for English language proficiency of foreign students. In *Testing the English proficiency of foreign students.* Washington, D.C.: Center for Applied Linguistics.

Cazabon, B. & Frenette, N. 1980, *Le français parle en situation minoritaire*, (Vol. 2): *L'enseignement du français parle, les manuels, les programmes, la formation des enseignants*. Toronto, Ontario: Ontario Ministry of Education.

1976 Census of Canada. Ottawa, Canada: Statistics, 1976.

Clark, J. L. D. 1972, *Foreign language testing: Theory and practice*. Philadelphia: The Center for Curriculum Development.

—— 1978, Psychometric considerations in language testing. In B. Spolsky (ed.), *Advances in language testing series, 2: Approaches to language testing.* Washington, D.C.: Center for Applied Linguistics.

—— 1980, Toward a common measure of speaking proficiency. In J. R. Frith (ed.), *Measuring spoken language proficiency.* Washington, D.C.: Georgetown University Press.

Cummins, J. in press, Is academic achievement distinguishable from language proficiency? In J. W. Oller, Jr. (ed.), *Current issues in language testing research.* Rowley, Mass.: Newbury House.

Cziko, G. 1981, Psychometric and edumetric approaches to language testing: Implications and applications. *Applied Linguistics*, 2(1), 27–44.

Farhady, H. 1980, *Justification, development and validation of functional language tests.* Unpublished doctoral dissertation, University of California at Los Angeles.

Fishman, J. & Cooper, R. L. 1978, The sociolinguistic foundations of language testing. In B. Spolsky (ed.), *Advances in language testing series, 2: Approaches to language testing.* Washington, D.C. Center for Applied Linguistics.

Hinofotis, F. B. 1981, Communicative competence in an educational environment: The relationship of quantifiable components. In J. Read (ed.), *Proceedings of the 15th Regional Language Center (RELC) Seminar on Evaluation and Measurement of Language Competence and Performance.* Singapore: Regional Language Center.

Hymes, D. H. 1967, Models of interaction of language and social setting. In J. Macnamara (ed.), *Problems of Bilingualism*, 23, 8–28. (Special issue of the *Journal of Social Issues*)

—— 1968, The ethnography of speaking. In J. Fishman (ed.), *Readings in the sociology of language.* The Hague: Mouton.

—— 1972, On communicative competence. In J. B. Pride & J. Holmes (eds), *Sociolinguistics.* Harmondsworth, England: Penguin Books.

Jones, R. L. 1977, Testing: A vital connection. In J. K. Phillips (ed.), *The language connection: From the classroom to the world.* Skokie, Ill. National Textbook Company.

—— 1979, The oral language interview of the Foreign Service Institute. In B. Spolsky (ed.), *Advances in language testing, Series 1: Some major tests.* Washington, D.C.: Center for Applied Linguistics.

—— 1981, Scoring procedures in oral language proficiency testing. In J. Read (ed.), *Proceedings of the 15th Regional Language Center (RELC) Seminar on Evaluation and Measurement of Language Competence and Performance.* Singapore: Regional Language Center.

Labov, W. 1969, The logic of nonstandard English. *Georgetown Monographs on Language and Linguistics*, 22, 1–31.

—— 1972, *Sociolinguistic patterns.* Philadelphia: University of Pennsylvania Press.

Lado, R. 1978, Scope and limitations of interview-based language testing: Are we asking too much of the interview? In J. L. D. Clark (ed.), *Direct testing of speaking proficiency: Theory and application.* Princeton, N.J.: Educational Testing Service.

Lepicq, D. 1980, *Aspects théoriques et empiriques de l'acceptabilité linguistique: Le cas du français des élèves des classes d'immersion.* Unpublished doctoral dissertation, University of Toronto.

McLean, L. D. 1980, *Separating the effect of more hours of instruction from general language development on achievement in French as a second language.* Paper presented at the Fourth International Symposium on Educational Testing, Antwerp, Belgium, June.

Morrow, K. E. 1977, *Techniques of evaluation for a notional syllabus.* University of Reading, London: Centre for Applied Language Studies. (Study commissioned by the Royal Society of Arts)

Mougeon, R. 1980, *Le français parlé en situation minoritaire* (Vol. 1). Toronto, Ontario: Ontario Ministry of Education.

Mougeon, R. & Canale, M. 1979, A linguistic perspective on Ontarian French. *Canadian Journal of Education,* 4(4), 59–65.

Oller, J. W., Jr. 1979, *Language tests at school.* London: Longman Group, Inc.

Oller, J. W., Jr. & Spolsky, B. 1979, The Test of English as a Foreign Language (TOEFL). In B. Spolsky (ed.), *Advances in language testing series, 1: Some major tests.* Washington, D.C.: Center for Applied Linguistics.

Ollivier, M. (ed.) 1962, *British North American Act: Selected Statutes, 1867–1962.* Ottawa, Canada: Queen's Printer.

Pike, L. 1973, *An evaluation of present and alternative item formats for use in the Test of English as a Foreign Language (TOEFL).* Princeton, N.J.: Educational Testing Service.

Shohamy, E. & Jorstod, H. L. 1980, *Students' attitudes toward testing: A consideration in test development and use.* Paper presented at the Northeast Conference on the Teaching of Foreign Languages, New York, April.

Spolsky, B. 1978, Introduction: Linguists and language testers. In B. Spolsky (ed.), *Advances in language testing series, 2: Approaches to language testing.* Washington, D.C.: Center for Applied Linguistics.

Swain, M. 1978, French immersion: Early, late or partial? *The Canadian Modern Language Review,* 34(3), 577–85.

Wesche, M. 1981, Communicative testing in a second language. *The Canadian Modern Language Review: Special issue in honor of H. H. Stern.*

Wiemann, J. M. & Backlund, P. 1980, Current theory and research in communicative competence. *Review of Educational Research,* 50(1), 185–199.

Wilds, C. P. 1975, The Oral Interview Test. In R. L. Jones & B. Spolsky (eds), *Testing language proficiency.* Arlington, VA: Center for Applied Linguistics.

The suitability of immersion education for children with special needs

Margaret Bruck, Ph.D.
McGill-Montreal Children's Hospital Learning Centre

Poor academic achievement of students is a common problem in all schools. Attempts to improve the poor performance of school-aged children involves, first, identifying the specific causes of school failure and then implementing a specific treatment program which best meets the needs of the individual student under consideration. Issues concerning valid diagnosis of and appropriate educational programming for the child with school problems are rarely straightforward. The situation becomes even more complex in the case of the child who is schooled in a second language. The purpose of this chapter is to provide a discussion of some of the current issues concerning the educational placement (vis-à-vis language of instruction) and the treatment of children educated in a second language who encounter school problems as a result of primary learning disabilities. The discussion is based on the results of several studies designed to determine whether education in a weaker language compounds specific disabilities or whether the same array of symptoms would appear if education occurred in the mother tongue.

The term specific learning disabilities refers to the characteristics of children who, along with many clearly intact abilities, show significant deficits in some areas of academic achievement. Although the predominant symptom of a learning disability is usually difficulty with learning to read, this may be accompanied by other difficulties such as physical awkwardness, directional disorientations, and the more familiar problems of spelling, math and written work. The persistent difficulties of these children cannot be attributed to mental retardation, emotional disturbance, sensory impairment, cultural disadvantage or lack of instruction. To date no neurological dysfunction has been identified which might account for the syndrome. In fact, what is most puzzling about the children is the lack of an adequate explanation for their failure to learn skills which other children acquire with apparent facility. Estimates of the prevalence of specific learning disabilities range from 10% to 20% of the school population.

Within the learning disabled population there are numbers of children who are called language disabled (LD). These are children who, despite physical well-being, normal intelligence and a healthy personality, acquire the first language with a painful slowness. They may be late in mastering the phonological patterns of their first language, in using words and combining them. They usually have difficulty in comprehending as well as producing speech. Because they lack facility in oral language at school age, they often miss the point of instructions, explanations and informal conversations. A language disability is usually sufficient cause for school difficulty. Recent estimates have indicated that 7% to 10% of the school age population exhibit some type of specific language learning problems.

Although it appears that a child with learning disabilities can never be "cured" (Silver & Hagin, 1964; Bruck, 1981), educational environments can be modified so that these children can remain in normal classrooms and can acquire sufficient levels of competence in the deficient skills to allow for academic success. In an attempt to offset years of academic failure and frustration, the early identification of learning disabilities is advanced by many so that such children will receive appropriate attention at as young an age as possible.

Methods for diagnosis and treatment of learning disabilities for the middle-class Anglophone child are much more straightforward than for the child schooled in a second language and/or from a minority background (Damico, Oller & Storey, 1981; Mercer, 1973; Cummins, 1980). In light of the fact that many minority children are diagnosed as "handicapped" when their primary difficulties lie in inadequate knowledge of the school language and/or the middle-class educational culture and, since there are at present no reliable or valid instruments to assess the primary problems of minority background children, there is a reluctance to attribute school failure to inherent psychological characteristics (e.g. low IQ, learning disability, etc.) of the minority child. Rather, the current favored diagnosis attributes failure to a poor match between the child and the requirements of the educational system. However, since the proportion of LD children is estimated to be 10% of the school population, and the incidence of Specific Learning Disabled (SLD) children is believed to be somewhat greater, one would expect to find similar incidence rates in various sub-populations. By avoiding proper identification, educators are actually preventing the minority child from receiving adequate treatment for his or her problems. In addition to the problems of diagnosis, the course of treatment for the SLD child from a minority background (whose mother tongue is not that of the school), or for the SLD child who has the option of being educated in two languages is more complicated than that for the majority culture child attending school in his mother tongue. A host of complex cultural, sociolinguistic and pedagogical issues commonly raised in the field of bilingual education, along with a number of additional concerns specific to the area of special education, must be considered. For example, should all instruction be in L1 until the SLD child has acquired sufficient competence in his mother tongue to benefit from instruction in L2? Should the SLD child be exposed to both L1 and L2 or will this dual system confuse the child who is slow to acquire basic skills in L1? Should the languages be temporally sequenced for literacy skills and/or for oral skills? In what language(s) should instruction be given? In addition to these psychological and pedagogical factors, one must also consider the sociolinguistic and cultural background of the child and attempt to place him or her in a situation where the mother tongue will not be replaced by the second language, and where pride in his own culture can be fostered. Social psychological factors should not take a secondary position to pedagogical-psychological considerations, for they are both crucial to the healthy development of all children.

At present, while these diagnostic and treatment issues remain unresolved and controversial for the minority child, there are some empirical data from several studies which address these issues in the case of the majority child. The children in these studies were from monolingual English speaking backgrounds in the Montreal area and attended French immersion programs. In this home-school language switch model, all instruction in the early primary grades is carried out in the second language, French. Although the children enter the program with no facility in French, they are taught all the basic literacy skills and academic skills in the second language. English is not introduced into the curriculum until the beginning of Grade II (Lambert & Tucker, 1972).

In the first study, kindergarten children attending French immersion programs were screened to identify a group of subjects with language disabilities. In addition, three comparison groups were identified children with language disabilities schooled in English, children with normal first language skills schooled in French immersion, and children with normal language skills schooled in English. Once the groups were selected, the linguistic cognitive, academic and second language skills of each subject were assessed annually from kindergarten until the end of Grade III (see

Bruck, 1978, 1982 for full details).
The data were examined to address the following issues:
1. Does exposure to a second language interfere with the LD child's acquisitions of first language skills?
2. Can LD children acquire oral proficiency in a second language?
3. Do LD children acquire oral proficiency in second language literacy skills?

The results will be briefly summarized:
1. Anglophone children with language disabilities attending French immersion programs acquired oral proficiency in their first language at the same rate as LD children schooled in their mother tongue. Thus, exposure to and instruction in a weaker language did not confuse these children nor impede their linguistic growth.
2. The LD children in French immersion acquired oral proficiency in French, although not at the same rate as French immersion children with normal development in the first language. However, in that the target group was delayed in acquiring oral competence in their first language, it would be unrealistic and paradoxical to expect them to acquire facility in the second language at the same rate as the control subjects. In contrast, it should be noted that the LD children in the English stream who followed a traditional French-as-a-second-language (FSL) program for 30 minutes a day over a period of three years had acquired no L2 skills.
   These data are consistent with those from other Canadian studies (e.g. Genesee, 1978; Lambert & Tucker, 1972; Swain & Barik, 1976) which have shown that the French immersion program is an efficient method for teaching second language skills especially when compared to traditional FSL classes. However, the present results indicate that this trend may be even more powerful for the LD child who fares particularly poorly in traditional second language courses where the major teaching methods stress repetition of linguistic utterances in non-meaningful contexts. The skills required to perform tasks, such as rote memory materials and good auditory skills, are often those that the LD child has specific problems with in his first language. Therefore, it is not surprising that so many of the control children with language disabilities did not benefit from traditional approaches to teaching a second language. However, as the present results indicate, given the appropriate conditions, children with poor first language skills can acquire oral proficiency in a second language.
3. In terms of academic skills (e.g. reading, spelling, math) the LD

immersion children were proceeding at the expected rate. They were learning these skills more slowly than normal children, but this was expected given their linguistic problems. Thus, having a language disability and being educated in a second language was not a double burden to these children.

A second study was designed to examine the effects of French immersion programs on a more heterogeneous group of learning disabled children (i.e. oral proficiency in and development of first language skills was normal for many of the subjects who nevertheless were delayed in the acquisition of reading and writing skills). The study also examined the effects of various educational interventions on the children's learning problems. Several groups of LD children with French immersion histories were studied:

— SLD children who transferred from a French immersion to an English program because it was felt by parents and educators that they would have fewer problems in the latter stream. After switching into the English stream many of these children received individualized remediation for their learning problems.

— SLD children who received all their elementary school education in the immersion stream. Many of these children received individualized remedial teaching in French (see Bruck, 1979, 1980, for further details).

Preliminary analysis of these data indicate:

1. Children who transferred to the English stream continued to have the same problems that were reported while in French immersion. Changing the language of instruction did not solve or alleviate their presenting problems.

2. Those children who made the most successful adjustments in the English stream were those who received the most intensive and individualized remedial help.

3. Similarly, children with problems who remained in the French stream, and who received remedial assistance in French for their problems fared particularly well.

These results suggest that SLD children will have similar academic problems irrespective of the language of instruction. Therefore, changing the language of instruction will not be an effective strategy for dealing with their school problems. Rather, these children require remedial assistance which directly teaches the specific skills which are lacking. Such programs can be carried out regardless of the language of the classroom.

While these data indicate that LD children from majority sociolinguistic backgrounds benefit from instruction in a second language, they cannot be directly generalized to situations where LD children from a minority background are schooled in a second language. While both groups of children may have similar types of learning disabilities and thus enter school without the necessary cognitive-linguistic prerequisities required for the acquisition of academic skills, the sociolinguistic factors describing their respective educational environments differentiate their experiences.

The majority background children described in the above studies have been educated in a particular home-school language switch program which promotes "additive" forms of bilingualism (Lambert, 1975). That is, while French (L2) is the only language of instruction in the early grades, there is still a great deal of cultural support and exposure to the first language which is highly valued in both the school and community. Furthermore, the first language is increasingly integrated into the curriculum so that by the end of Grade IV both languages are equally represented in the program. Most minority children, on the other hand, attend schools which promote "subtractive" forms of bilingualism. That is, either the child's first language is never used as a medium of instruction or, when it is, the first language is gradually replaced by a more prestigious second language. For these situations, the data on the majority child are not relevant. However, in the case of the minority child who attends a bilingual program, the goals of which are to value and promote first language skills, the data from the Canadian studies suggest the manner in which SLD children would perform in bilingual classrooms. This information may have important implications for the improvement of such programs for the SLD minority child. The following is a discussion of certain themes which are relevant to the minority situation in this context.

First, the data indicate that under certain conditions children with low levels of L1 competence can acquire a second language without suffering academic or cognitive impairment. The data endorse the position that cultural, sociolinguistic and pedagogical factors in the school and community are more important than the learner's cognitive-linguistic abilities in predicting the success of bilingual education environments (cf. Cummins, 1979). Thus, one should not be concerned that exposing the LD minority child to a second language *per se* will have negative effects on various aspects of his or her development. Rather, one would expect that the SLD minority child would profit from second language instruction in those situations where the first language is maintained, where teachers have positive attitudes toward the student's level of second language achievement, native language and culture. Instruction should also include a situation in which the level of second language instruction is geared towards the student's initially low level of competence in that language (cf.

Cohen & Swain, 1976). Because many bilingual programs have been designed to fulfil these conditions which are absent in English mainstream schools, one would therefore opt to place the SLD minority child in these programs.

Second, because the children under consideration do have specific learning disabilities, they will be slower than the average child to acquire oral and written skills in the first and second languages. As a result, educators and parents should not interpret lower achievement levels as evidence that the bilingual programs have failed; rather, it should be recognized that these children have specific underlying difficulties which will affect their performance regardless of the language of instruction.

Third, while some form of bilingual education is advocated for the SLD minority child, there are certain aspects of the curriculum which might have to be modified if such children are to maximally benefit from their educational experiences. One area involves the teaching of literacy skills in L1 and L2. In many bilingual programs, beginning readers receive instruction in the two codes concurrently. While the pedagogical soundness of this procedure has been questioned for the average child, it appears to be particularly inappropriate for the SLD child. In the French immersion setting the SLD children do acquire literacy skills in French and English, but the teaching of the two codes is carefully sequenced. The immersion children are first taught all basic literacy skills in French, the second language. After two years of total L2 instruction, English is introduced into the curriculum and similar skills are then taught in L1. Most of the students acquire the fundamentals of L2 literacy skills before English is presented and easily transfer skills from one language to another. However, for the child who is slower to acquire basic reading skills, the above timetable for sequencing language of instruction is inappropriate. Typically, in such cases when reading instruction is given in English before the child has mastered the basic skills in French, confusion ensues. The child now seems to have more difficulty in French reading than he did before English was taught and, furthermore, is not able to "unlock" the English code. Many of these children eventually sort the situation out by themselves, but it appears to be an unnecessary burden which could be avoided by some simple modifications in the curriculum. Consequently, in clinical work done with the SLD immersion child, teachers are frequently asked to delay the introduction of English reading for such students until they demonstrate some facility in the French written code. When these suggestions are followed, the children show less confusion and eventually acquire better literacy skills in French and English than those SLD children who are taught English skills earlier in their career. Similar recommendations are proposed for the SLD minority child in a bilingual program who is just starting to read. These children should initially be given reading instruction in one language. Once they have demonstrated a good understanding of the process, they should be taught the same skills in a second language.

Another curricular concern involves the teaching of English as a second language. Research data indicates that second language programs based upon audiolingual methods are particularly ineffective techniques for teaching language skills to the SLD child. These children do not benefit from instructional methods which emphasize drills, memorization of specific language patterns and the use of language patterns in nonmeaningful contexts. New approaches are required which perhaps do not explicitly teach the target language but rather use it as a medium of instruction in more naturalistic communicative environments.

Finally, children who have learning disabilities require good remedial services which are well-designed to fit the individual needs of the learner. These programs involve helping the child to develop some of the skills on which reading, writing and arithmetic depend. A good program also involves making modifications in the classroom so that the child can profit from normal instruction and not become totally overwhelmed and frustrated by his daily academic experiences (e.g. reducing the homework load, providing letter strips and multiplication tables, etc.). These services are not interchangeable with bilingual education programs; they are independent components of the educational environment, each having very different aims and pedagogical approaches. Nor are these services mutually exclusive in that the best program for the SLD minority child should entail placement in a bilingual classroom which offers the appropriate remedial services.

Conclusions

While similar studies must be carried out in the American context to corroborate the findings of the Canadian immersion studies, the data from the studies cited suggest the feasibility of educating LD children in "additive" bilingual environments. Given the appropriate pedagogical and social psychological conditions such students can learn a second language without impeding normal development of first language and cognitive academic skills. However, bilingual education by itself is not a solution for their specific learning problems. These children require the same special attention given to LD children who are educated in their first language. By denying them such help, educators are not only doing a disservice to the individual child, but also to the bilingual program itself. Bilingual programs should not be viewed as a special education service. Rather, they should provide an environment where children, regardless of their academic or cognitive potential, can acquire proficiency in two languages and knowledge of two cultures while maintaining their respective ethnic identities.

References

Bruck, M. 1978, The suitability of early French immersion programs for the language disabled child. *Canadian Journal of Education*, 3, 51–72.
—— 1979, Switching out of French immersion. *Interchange*, 9, 86–94.
—— 1980, *Consequences of switching children out of French immersion: A pilot study*. Report submitted to the Quebec Ministry of Education.
—— 1981, *A follow-up of learning disabled children into late adolescence and young adulthood*. Unpublished manuscript, McGill-Montreal Children's Hospital Learning Centre.
—— 1982, Language impaired child performance in an additive bilingual educational program. *Applied Psycholinguistics*, 3(1).
Cohen, A. D. & Swain, M. 1976, Bilingual education: The immersion model in the North American context. *TESOL Quarterly*, 10, 45–53.
Cummins, J. 1979, Linguistic interdependence and the educational development of bilingual children. *Review of Educational Research*, 49(2), 222–51.
—— 1980, *Psychological assessment of minority language students* (Final Report). Ontario Institute for Studies in Education.
Damico, J., Oller, J. W. & Storey, M. E. 1981, The diagnosis of language disorders in bilingual children: Pragmatic and surface-oriented criteria. In J. Erickson & D. Omark (eds), *The bilingual exceptional child*. Springfield, Ill.: Charles C. Thomas.
Genesee, F. 1978, A longitudinal evaluation of an early immersion school program. *Canadian Journal of Education*, 3, 31–50.
Lambert, W. E. 1975, Culture and language as factors in learning and education. In A. Wolfgang (ed.), *Education of immigrant students*. Toronto: Ontario Institute for Studies in Education.
Lambert, W. & Tucker, G. R. 1972, *The bilingual education of children: The St. Lambert experiment*. Rowley, Mass: Newbury House.
Mercer, J. 1973, *Labelling the mentally retarded*. Berkeley: University of California Press.
Silver, A. A. & Hagin, R. A. 1964, Specific reading disability: Follow-up studies. *American Journal of Orthopsychiatry*, 34, 95–102.
Swain, M. & Barik, H. C. 1976, Bilingual education for the English Canadian: Recent developments. In A. Simoes (ed.), *The bilingual child: Research and analysis of existing educational themes*. New York: Academic Press.

Conclusion

Psycholinguistic aspects

Fred Genesee
McGill University

"Despite the enormous amount of research on child language for the last two decades, the fundamental question of 'what must the child learn in order to master his language?' has not been adequately answered. Most investigators have concentrated on the child's acquisition of the phonological, syntactic and semantic structures of linguistic competence. But it is becoming increasingly clearer that language acquisition involves more than learning grammar . . . it is unarguable that he must also be learning how to use utterances appropriately in actual situations" (Dore, 1979, p. 227).

Indeed, in recent years psycholinguistic research and theorizing has undergone a major shift away from issues concerning grammatical competence, as conceptualized by structuralist and transformational grammarians, toward issues related to communicative competence and certain aspects of performance that were vigorously avoided by earlier scholars.
   It is interesting to note that while there has been a similar shift away from an exclusively structuralist, grammar-based orientation in the area of second language teaching, the full implications of a communicative approach to language acquisition have not yet been felt in theories of second language acquisition. No extant theories of second language acquisition have seriously considered the effects of being communicatively competent in one language on the acquisition of another. Albeit second language researchers have certainly discussed and examined the significance of transfer from one language to another, they have considered primarily transfer of language structures, be they phonological, lexical, or syntactic.
   The shift toward communication-based models of language acquisition in the first language field has certainly had an impact on second language pedagogy, however. One of the most publicized and striking examples of

this is the Canadian French immersion programs which are based on models of first language acquisition and are designed to enhance second language learning by promoting meaningful interpersonal communication in the second language (Genesee, 1983). Other, less extreme but nonetheless important examples can be found in the communication-based foreign or second language programs that are now offered in many Canadian and American public schools (see Savignon, 1972, for example).

Language proficiency assessment has been a major preoccupation of bilingual educators concerned with the education of language minority children in the U.S. A basic tenet of bilingual education is that such children cannot benefit fully from the advantages of academic tuition so long as they lack proficiency in the language of instruction. Therefore, it follows that children who are not native speakers of English, the usual language of instruction in most American schools, should be educated in their native language until such time as they acquire the requisite proficiency in English. Decisions regarding entry to and exit from bilingual education programs have thus required assessment of the children's language proficiencies. Legislative events as well have played no trivial role in defining language proficiency as the critical variable in bilingual education to the virtual exclusion of other factors.

It is argued that traditional language assessment procedures are ineffective and invalid in making entry and exit decisions because they do not assess the child's proficiency in using language in familiar and realistic social contexts. It has also been pointed out that by failing to take into account the child's language proficiency in different contexts (school and non-school related) conventional assessment instruments fail to adequately characterize the language minority child's full range of language skills. In light of the apparent inadequacy of traditional language proficiency tests for language minority children, and in light of current communicative competence approaches to both first and second language learning, it is not surprising that bilingual educators are turning to theories of communicative competence to better satisfy their assessment needs.

Simply stated, it is believed that effective educational placement of language minority children, and possibly even their ultimate academic success, is a function of their communicative competence in the language of instruction. It must be stressed that this relationship is stated *simply,* since bilingual educators have clearly and frequently discussed the importance of other factors, most notably cultural. It seems permissible and appropriate, however, to restrict discussion here to language *per se*, at least for the moment.

The emphasis on communicative competence in designing and making educational decisions about educational programs for language minority children reflects a strong professional belief, as well as a serious commitment in time and money, that such an approach will be successful in defining the needs of these children. Underlying this belief is a number of assumptions that significantly affect its tenability and, therefore, warrant discussion. Four assumptions that can be identified are:

1. communicative competence can be characterized;
2. communicative competence can be assessed;
3. communicative competence can be taught; and
4. communicative competence is in fact related in a significant way to academic achievement.

Each of these assumptions will be considered in turn.

Assumption 1: Communicative competence can be characterized

Despite all the attention being devoted to developing a model of communicative competence there is considerable debate over the precise form that such a model should take (see Canale & Swain, 1980, for a review of the second language literature). In particular, there is as yet no consensus concerning the types of competencies that should be included in such a model. Some theorists, such as Hymes (1972), include grammatical competence, that is knowledge of the structure of a given language, along with sociolinguistic competence, that is knowledge underlying its effective and appropriate use. Canale & Swain (1980) have argued in favour of also including strategic competence, that is verbal and non-verbal communication strategies that may be used to compensate for lack of competence in grammatical rules. Others accept a definition of communicative competence that refers to the ability to successfully transmit messages using any means, linguistic and non-linguistic, without regard for their grammaticality or sociolinguistic appropriateness (Savignon, 1972; Schultz, 1977). Yet others maintain that the distinction between grammatical or linguistic competence and sociolinguistic competence is ill-founded. Connors (1980) contends that the two are linguistically indissociable and that evidence of their distinctiveness actually reflects differences between language and non-language-based proficiencies. Without delving further into this thorny theoretical debate, which seems far from being resolved, the point is fairly clear. A comprehensive, widely acceptable use of the notion of communicative competence as a basis for language proficiency assessment in bilingual education awaits a resolution of these issues.

In the meantime, even if the theoretical distinction between gramma-

tical and sociolinguistic competence were accepted as minimum components in a model of communicative competence, two fundamental issues
remain. The first concerns the identification and description of the
language functions that constitute communicative competence. In this
regard, Wilkins (1977, p. 23) points out that "while there has been quite
enough scholarly discussion of semantics and grammatical categories for
there to be little that is contentious in a list of candidates for inclusion in a
semantic-grammatical inventory, there is no comparable authority for
establishing a universal set of categories of language use." Lists of language
functions have been prepared for pedagogical purposes (see, for example,
Wilkins, 1977), but it must be admitted that these are in fact ad hoc. There
is as yet no empirical or theoretical justification for the items in these lists,
nor does such justification appear imminent.

The second issue concerns the specification of the linguistic structures
that are necessary to perform designated language functions in a sociolinguistically appropriate fashion; in other words, the formulation of a
grammar of communication. Connors points out that it is probably
impossible to formulate such a grammar in the present state of our
knowledge and in view of the intuitive way in which language functions
have been constructed. Extant grammars are likely to offer little guidance
in this regard because they have been formulated on intuitive, asocial and
non-functional grounds. The best that can be achieved at this time perhaps
is an empirical description of the linguistic structures that a sample of
native speakers use to realize particular functions in certain social situations. How the relationship between the structures thus identified and their
respective functions are described is an open question.

It might be argued at this point that although the task of attempting to
describe the core language functions that constitute overall communicative
competence and the linguistic structures needed to perform them is
gargantuan, it is manageable if one were to limit investigation to classroom
use of language. Indeed, this is probably true, at least from an empirical
point of view. Some bilingual educators and theoreticians, however,
contend that appropriate educational decisions about language minority
children can be made only if their communicative competence in extra-
curricular settings is also assessed. In this case, any simplification gained by
restricting language assessment to classroom contexts would be lost.

Even within the social limits imposed by classroom interactions,
however, the problem of teacher and classroom variation would still have
to be addressed. Could it be assumed that what constitutes core language
functions and communicative competence in one classroom applies to
another classroom? Variations in communicative competence associated

with different grade levels would need to be considered as well: Are the communicative competencies required at successively higher grade levels cumulative, or are they disjunctive in some way? This latter question is of some importance for bilingual educators who are required to deal with language minority children at different ages. Furthermore, would the bilingual educator interested in communicative competence and the language minority child need to characterize his or her competence in both the first and second languages? This of course would depend upon the particular model of bilingual education that is being considered. All of these questions require careful empirical examination.

In sum, a number of fundamental issues concerning the nature of communicative competence in general and in the classroom in particular are outstanding. The overriding question is whether answers to these issues are necessary if communicative models of language proficiency can presently be applied meaningfully and usefully in bilingual education.

Assumption 2: Communicative competence can be assessed

At least three major issues face test developers working in communicative competence: (1) the authenticity or face validity of communicative competence tests; (2) their representativeness or situational generalizability; and (3) the definition of proficiency levels.

Authenticity. Although there is as yet little consensus regarding the exact nature of communicative competence, as has already been discussed, it is nevertheless generally accepted that real communication is dynamic, interactive, and often even unpredictable. The question then arises as to how these features of real communication can be incorporated into the testing situation. It is felt that most existing language proficiency tests, which are usually highly structured and of the discrete-point variety, do not involve genuine communication but rather "artificial, language-like behavior" (Carroll, 1980, p. 12). It has been suggested that the development of direct, integrative language proficiency tests would circumvent the problem of artificiality posed by indirect, discrete-point methods (Carroll, 1980; Clark, 1972).

While it is true that direct tests, such as the *Foreign Service Institute Oral Proficiency Test* (FSI, 1970), have considerable face validity, there are problems associated with these techniques. In contrast to most discrete-point tests that can be scored by relatively untrained people, or even by computer, using objective criteria, scoring of direct tests generally requires highly trained personnel. The widespread use of communicative tests by school personnel in the educational system would thus pose considerable training problems. The requirement that most direct tests of communicative competence be administered individually, in order to achieve authenticity, poses an additional problem in educational settings where large numbers of students may have to be assessed. The viability and utility of any testing program depends on its being practical and efficient.

Canale & Swain (1980) have made a distinction between communicative competence and communicative performance that is useful here. They define the former as the relationship between grammatical competence, or knowledge of the rules of grammar, and sociolinguistic competence, or knowledge of the rules of language use. Performance is defined as the realization of these competencies and their interaction in the actual production and comprehension of utterances. Whereas the assessment of communicative performance might require authentic integrative testing, with all of the problems associated with this approach, the assessment of communicative competence may be achieved fairly satisfactorily with indirect, discrete-point testing that is communication-based. To the extent that competence correlates with performance, the problems inherent in the latter could be avoided. To date, however, even tests of communicative competence in Canale & Swain's sense have not been developed.

Situational generalizability. An additional characteristic of real communication that is of some concern to test developers is its situational diversity. Until proven otherwise, it cannot be assumed that competence in one situation is associated with competence in other situations, even those that might be situationally similar: For example, a child's ability to communicate effectively in teacher-student interactions in contrast to student-student interactions. From the test developer's perspective the issue here is how to assess efficiently and effectively communicative competence/performance in diverse social domains/situations. A comprehensive test of communicative competence must necessarily reflect such diversity. Therefore, it is unlikely that an assessment of communicative competence will consist of one test; it is likely to require many, each reflecting sociolinguistically-distinct situations within a particular setting. The number and nature of language functions that constitute communicative competence in different situations is an empirical question. Indeed, the number and nature of distinct situations is also an important outstanding question. A number of researchers are presently investigating this issue in the classroom.

Definition of proficiency levels. It is in the definition of proficiency levels that theories of communicative competence face their most imposing problem. Tests of communicative competence/performance are not concerned so much with correctness as they are with appropriateness — that is, what set of linguistic structures are necessary or sufficient to realize particular language functions in sociolinguistically appropriate ways. As has already been pointed out, it is probably not possible at present to map grammatical structures onto language functions in any systematic way given the relatively undeveloped state of educators' knowledge about language functions. Lacking such linguistic descriptions, empirical descriptions could nevertheless be established of the types of linguistic structures that native speakers habitually use to realize particular language functions in given social situations. Proficiency levels might then be defined according to the relative frequency of occurrence of specific structures. Use of this approach, which is essentially a normative one, runs counter to the frequently voiced suggestion that criterion-referenced testing be used in assessing communicative competence. Furthermore, such an approach is not very heuristic and tends toward a listing of utterances to be used to fulfill particular functions.

Even this empirical approach, which seems practical, and conceptually reasonable, albeit demanding, is problematic. When selecting a norming group, should one use any and all native speakers, only academically successful native speakers, or native speakers who differ systematically with respect to academic achievement. Are native speakers, in fact, the appropriate norming group? Canale & Swain (1980, p. 12) point out that native-speaking interlocutors may be more tolerant toward grammatical and stylistic (i.e. sociolinguistic) "failures" in the language of second language speakers than native speakers. The implication here is that native English-speaking teachers may be less demanding of language minority students than of native English-speaking students. Thus the use of native English speakers as a norming group when establishing acceptable English proficiency levels for bilingual education may consistitute an unrealistically high standard. If one were to establish proficiency levels using non-native speakers, which non-native speakers should one use?

The challenges inherent in assessing communicative competence are no less formidable than those encountered in developing a model of communicative competence. The state of communicative competence testing is perhaps best exemplified by B. J. Carroll's assertion that "it is unfortunate that the adventurous thinking taking place in the field of applied linguistics, communication and sociolinguistics is not being matched in the field of testing" (1980, p. 90).

Assumption 3: Communicative competence can be taught

The emphasis on communicative competence testing as a basis for entry and exit decisions in bilingual education rests on the expectation that children lacking the requisite competence in English can be taught the necessary skills while receiving other educational instruction in the native language. Once the necessary competence has been achieved, the children can be integrated into an English program of instruction. A review of much of the literature on psycholinguistics would give the impression that a theoretical basis for developing rational programs of communicative competence training is lacking. Our understanding of the actual processes underlying children's acquisition of communicative competence in the first language is still quite incomplete despite considerable research during recent years. An understanding of the process of second language learning is even more inconclusive, in part, perhaps, because the task confronting the second language researcher is complicated by a greater diversity of learner characteristics and learning conditions in the case of second language learning.

At the same time, it must be admitted that considerable progress has been made in describing the *conditions* surrounding normal first language acquisition. In particular, research begun some 10 years ago by Catherine Snow (1972) on mothers' talk to children, and subsequently pursued in various ways by many others (see Snow & Ferguson, 1977, for a review of this work), has advanced knowledge of the language models that first language learners are exposed to. The nature and significance of second language input for the second language learner has also become a subject of recent empirical investigation (Freed, 1981; Hamayan & Tucker, 1980; Krashen, 1981). Although there is much theoretical discussion about the precise functions and consequences of "caretaker language" on language acquisition (Clark & Clark, 1977), this research is instructive in describing the social and linguistic conditions that accompany first language acquisition. It thus becomes possible to use this information to re-create the conditions characteristic of first language acquisition in order to promote second language learning.

Indeed, the results of evaluations of communicatively-oriented programs of second language instruction indicate that they are markedly better than grammar-based programs at fostering communicative proficiency. Research on the Canadian immersion programs attests to the benefits in overall communicative proficiency that can be realized in second language programs that are oriented to communication (Genesee, 1978). Research by Savignon (1972) with American college-age students enrolled in an introductory audio-lingual French course demonstrates that students can successfully learn specific communicative skills provided their syllabus includes at least some training in the use of those skills. In contrast, other groups of students enrolled in similar audio-lingual programs lacking the communication skills component did not acquire proficiency in these skills.

How successful programs of communicative competence are judged to be may be less a matter of the students' actual communicative proficiency as defined in some externally objective way, and more a matter of teachers' and evaluators' expectations and tolerance with regard to what constitutes acceptable levels of proficiency. The Canadian immersion programs are a case in point. Immersion students are perceived by most involved to be successful second language learners despite considerable grammatical inaccuracies (Adiv, 1980) and what might be regarded as a lack of sociolinguistic sophistication in the use of their second language (Connors, 1980). It is also patently clear from numerous evaluations that immersion students acquire the communication skills required for scholastic performance and that they use their acquired competence successfully in school learning (Genesee, 1982). Were the immersion teachers less tolerant with regard to the students' second language competence, this might be expected to have a dampening effect on their use of the second language in the pursuit of academic goals, thereby jeopardizing their overall academic progress. This does not happen, in large part, it could be argued, because of the teachers' tolerance of the students' communicative competence in the second language.

The results from the immersion programs are also instructive in illustrating the levels of communicative competence that can be attained within an educational setting. It is quite possible that immersion students' communicative competence is relatively less adequate in non-academic settings than in academic settings, although no real examination of this possibility has been undertaken. Were this found to be the case, it should not be viewed as a failing of the immersion program, but rather as a statement on how much communicative competence should reasonably be expected to occur within the rather severe social constraints imposed by schools. The task of acquiring complete communicative competence cannot be accomplished within schools alone; extra-school support and experiences in the target language are necessary.

Thus, notwithstanding the lack of sound theoretical bases for expecting communication skills training to work, in fact communication-oriented educational programs have been found to be relatively successful at least within the limits set by school settings. It has been suggested that such programs achieve their success possibly by directing educators' attention away from an exclusive concern for correct grammatical usage and toward real communication, without which the business of language acquisition cannot take place.

Assumption 4: Communicative competence is related in a significant way to academic achievement

The emphasis on communicative competence in current thinking about the education of language minority children assumes that such competence plays a primary role in academic achievement. While it is probably true that some minimal competence in the language of instruction is necessary for learning to occur, it is unlikely that it is sufficient to insure learning. Learning is an extremely complex process involving sociocultural factors, cognitive factors, the motivational and affective state of the learner and teacher, as well as the general physiological well-being of the learner. The language minority child may not respond to efforts to educate him or her for motivational, attitudinal or other reasons irrespective of his or her actual communicative competence in the language of instruction. Indeed, the very acquisition of communicative competence itself may depend upon these factors as well. Research by Hamayan and Genesee (Genesee & Hamayan, 1980) on individual difference in second language learning among young Anglophone children demonstrates how complex the relationship between second language learning and selected psychological characteristics of the learner can be. Troike (1978) has outlined and underlined some well-documented sociocultural aspects of language proficiency. And recent research on the social psychology of language has drawn attention to the important role that language plays as a symbol of ethnic identity, especially in cross-cultural encounters (Giles, Robinson, & Smith, 1980). These diverse lines of inquiry suggest potential sources of influence that should figure prominently in any program of educational intervention for language minority children along with the strictly communicative bias that characterizes much of the intervention programs. However, before this can be accomplished, systematic investigations into the precise role and relationships of these factors need to be undertaken in the context of bilingual education. Some progress is being made in this direction with the assistance of grants from the National Institute of Education to study the characteristics that distinguish successful bilingual programs (Tikunoff *et. al.*, 1980). Similar research at the level of the learner and teacher needs to be undertaken to complement the N.I.E. project.

What is at issue here is not whether language competence alone is or is not related to academic achievement but rather to what extent and in what ways. Greater attention needs to be paid to the potential influence of other non- and paralinguistic factors, alone and in interaction with language proficiency. A multi-dimensional approach of this sort seems more likely to correspond to the multidimensional complexity of the problems educators are facing.

Summary

The notion of communicative competence is a major theme of this volume.

A number of assumptions underlying the use of this notion in the assessment of minority language children's language proficiency have been identified and discussed.

In particular, it was pointed out that as yet unresolved theoretical and psychometric issues pose formidable challenges to the implementation of communicative testing in bilingual education. Notwithstanding these challenges, it is evident that if language assessment techniques are to keep stride with evolving perspectives in linguistics, sociolinguistics and psychology, they will necessarily have to incorporate aspects of communication, however ultimately defined. Recent writings by B. J. Caroll (1980), Mumby (1978) and Wesche (1981) attest to the progress being made in communicative competence test development. It should not be unexpected that there appear to be intractable problems obstructing rapid progress in this field since real communication involves no less than all those factors and processes associated with individuals engaged in interpersonal encounters situated in diverse social settings. Indeed, the very complexity of the problems reviewed here suggests that we are in fact moving in the right direction.

References

Adiv, E. 1980, *An analysis of second language performance in two types of immersion programs.* Unpublished doctoral dissertation, Department of Education in Second Languages, McGill University.

Canale, M. & Swain, M. 1980, Theoretical bases of communicative approaches to second language teaching and testing. *Applied Linguistics,* 1, 1–47.

Carroll, B. J. 1980, *Testing communicative performance: An interim study.* Oxford: Pergamon Press.

Clark, H. H. & Clark, E. V. 1977, *Language and psychology.* New York: Harcourt, Brace & Jovanovich.

Clark, J. L. D. 1972, *Foreign language testing: Theory and practice.* Philadelphia: The Center for Curriculum Development.

Connors, K. 1980, Grammatical versus communicative competence in second language learning: A view from linguistics. *Canadian Journal of Psychology,* 34, 328–36.

Dore, J. 1979, Conversational acts and the acquisition of language. In E. Ochs & B. Schieffelin (eds), *Developmental pragmatics*. NY: Academic Press, 339–61.

Foreign Service Institute (FSI) — Educational Testing Service (ETS). 1970, Foreign Service Institute Oral Interview Test. In *Manual for Peace Corps language testers*. Princeton, N.J.: ETS.

Freed, B. 1981, Talking to foreigners versus talking to children: Similarities and differences. In R. C. Scarcella & S. D. Krashen (eds), *Research in second language acquisition*. Rowley, Mass.: Newbury House.

Genesee, F. 1978, A longitudinal evaluation of an early immersion school program. *Canadian Journal of Education*, 3, 31–50.

—— 1982, Bilingual education of majority language children: The immersion experiments in review. *Applied Psycholinguistics*.

Genesee, F. & Hamayan, E. 1980, Individual differences in second language learning. *Applied Psycholinguistics*, 1, 95–110.

Giles, H., Robinson, W. P. & Smith, P. M. (eds) 1980, *Language: Social psychological perspectives*. Oxford: Pergamon Press.

Hamayan, E. & Tucker, G. R. 1980, Language input in the classroom and its relationship to second language achievement. *TESOL Quarterly*, 14, 453-68.

Hymes, D. 1972, On communicative competence. In J. B. Pride & J. Holmes (eds), *Sociolinguistics*. Harmondsworth, England: Penguin Books.

Krashen, S. 1981, The theoretical and practical relevance of simple codes in second language acquisition. In R. C. Scarcella & S. D. Krashen (eds), *Research in second language acquisition*. Rowley, Mass.: Newbury House.

Mumby, J. 1978, *Communicative syllabus design*. Cambridge: Cambridge University Press.

Savignon, S. 1972, *Communicative competence: An experiment in foreign language teaching*. Philadelphia: The Center for Curriculum Development.

Schultz, R. A. 1977, Discrete-point versus simulated communication testing in foreign languages. *The Modern Language Journal*, 61, 94–100.

Snow, C. E. 1972, Mother's speech to children learning language. *Child Development*, 43, 549–65.

Snow, C. E. & Ferguson, G. A. 1977, *Talking to children: Language input and acquisition*. Cambridge: Cambridge University Press.

Tikunoff, W. K., Ward, B. A., Fisher, C. A., Armendariz, J., Parker, L., Dominguez, D., Vazquez, J. A., Mercado, C., Romero, M., Good, T. A. 1980, *Descriptive Study of Significant Bilingual Instructional Features*. Far West Laboratory for Educational Research and Development, San Francisco, Ca., March.

Troike, R. 1978, Research evidence for the effectiveness of bilingual education. *NABE Journal*, 3, 13–24.

Wesche, M. B. 1981, Communicative testing in a second language. *The Canadian Modern Language Review*, 37(3), 551-71.

Wilkins, D. A. 1977, *Notional syllabuses*. Oxford: Oxford University Press.

Index

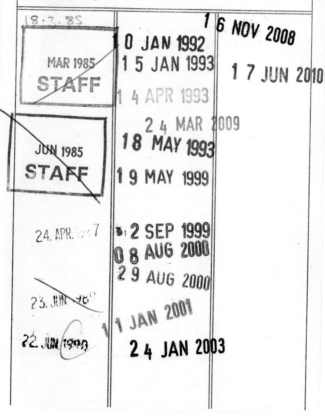